THIS THERAPIST LIKES TO PL

In this game, there are **no rules**

THIS

A

THERAPIST

Terrifying

LIKES TO

True Story

PLAY

Suzanne Joubert

Published in 2023 by Suzanne Joubert, Cork, Ireland.
Copyright © 2023 Suzanne Joubert

ISBN (paperback) 978-1399-96-348-0
ISBN (ebook) 978-1399-96-396-1

Cover Design and Interior Layout by designforwriters.com

This book is a memoir. It reflects the author's present recollections of experiences over time. All names of the characters in this book have been changed and given a pseudonym which conceals their identity. The only exception to this is Don Hennessey, who has given the author written permission for his name and a full rendering of our work together to be mentioned in this book.

Each event described is factual and can be verified by research. Dialogue and phrases with each character are consistent with the character, but do not represent word-for-word written transcripts. The essence of the dialogue is accurate. Place names are real. TK Logan has given written consent to the author to mention her work on Proxy Stalking, including the brief quotes mentioned in the book.

Contents

Part 1: A Change in the Air

Part Two: This Therapist Likes to Play

Part Three: The Real Suzanne

Part Four: Unsilencing

There is a secret.

A clandestine secret that draws people together, united in a common cause.

A game has been constructed: they like to play with their victims.

Cat and mouse, predator and prey.

They are predators. Other people are their prey.

They carry with them rage, delusions, a wish to be pseudocommando.

With this delusion comes certainty. A deep, unshakeable resolve to hurt, to commit violence.

They start with their own secret issues.

They become a group.

They become more organized.

This secret, this clandestine operation, makes them feel better about themselves.

They become more violent.

They become a large underworld network.

All players are united in the Dark Tetrad:

Machiavellianism

Narcissism

Psychopathy

Sadism

PART 1:
A CHANGE IN THE AIR

'Victimization by Proxy stalkers (Multiple Perpetrators of Stalking) could represent heightened consequences for victims, as having multiple people watching, following, or harassing them could intensify their feelings of fear and worry, and indicates their primary stalker is committed to continuing the relationship.

'Stalking tactics generally meant to keep the stalker informed of the victim's daily activities are associated with a higher risk of physical violence and homicide among stalking victims, and it is normally where Proxy Stalking takes place.'

Logan & Walker[1]

---

1   Logan, T. K., & Walker, R. (2017). 'Stalking: A multidimensional framework for assessment and safety planning.' *Trauma, Violence, & Abuse*, 18(2), 200–222.

THE EXPERIMENT

Imagine waking up one morning, looking out of the window with a cup of coffee in your hand, to find yourself at the centre of a social experiment.

A cat-and-mouse game has been constructed; you are the mouse. It's a game to see how far you will go and how far you can be pushed before you break.

Your world is slowly ripped apart. Lies about you start spreading.

People start following you, intruding on your life wherever you go. People break into your house, repeatedly, and the relevant authorities do nothing to protect you. You are constantly under surveillance.

Time and time again, you are harmed in every way possible, violently tormented by the players. The game that is being played is sadistic and dangerous.

It becomes impossible to continue your work, and your career is ruined. Your bank account empties. Slowly, day by day, you feel like your world is imploding, and you become increasingly isolated and trapped.

For four years you try to convince the authorities that something sinister is happening. It started with one person stalking you; now he has raised an army. Proxy stalking.

Attempts at explaining how you were being stalked are met with scorn and derision, time and time again. You visit the police forty-two times, yet still nothing is done.

Imagine that you live in a country where there are no laws against stalking, and no understanding of it.

Finally, imagine that this experiment was started and carried out by a registered therapist and counsellor, a profession that, as yet, has no statutory regulation in Ireland.

The counselling profession is self-regulated, and makes its own rules. It is a law unto itself.

If this was happening to you, what would you do?

A NORMAL LIFE

Before it all began, I had a normal, happy life.

I lived in East Cork, just outside the city, in a coastal village that was quaint and pretty, with a harbour at the foot of the village, and a large community hall at the top of the hill.

I had a small house, on a small estate. I said hello to neighbours and they said hello to me. I spoke to the elderly couple beside me, mostly about plants and gardening. I bought them chocolates; they helped me trim the hedge. I belonged to a yoga group, meeting weekly in the GAA hall nestled in the woods. We would meet for coffee in the local shop. Seated around the small square tables, we would exchange news and bits of local gossip.

I belonged to a walking group and a running group, meeting for a slow, ponderous jog around the town nearby. And I belonged to a music group, playing late into the night, in an old wooden barn lit by candles.

My life was full and busy, and I liked it that way. I was doing a Masters in Psychotherapy and seeing clients, and at the end of the week I would meet a friend down at the local pub. The community surrounding me was vibrant. There were times when I felt lonely, but I was always surrounded by people and that took the edge off the loneliness when it surfaced.

It wasn't a remarkable life, but it was a life I enjoyed, and I appreciated all the people in it. Weekends were spent doing things I liked, and sometimes doing very little at all. I often met with colleagues during conferences or training sessions,

9

and enjoyed the warm circle of friendship and camaraderie that existed around me.

It was the autumn of 2019 that my peaceful existence was shattered. It seems like a lifetime ago. Looking back, I see how the shape of my life has changed. Like a strong wind that catches a bird's nest and throws it far from the tops of the tallest tree; it rises into the sky, whirling, dizzy, and smashes into the earth far, far below.

In order to start at the very beginning, though, I need to go back to the autumn of 2015.

My therapy practice at that time was alongside another counsellor's office up a narrow staircase, just off the main street in the middle of a nearby town. The counsellor, Paul, was a small, narrow man with badly fitting jeans and a gap between his teeth.

After a while, the rent of my rather large office space increased and I wondered what to do. At that point, I was knee-deep in my studies and finances were already stretched.

'You can share my room,' said Paul. He invited me to join a counselling supervision group. 'It's a great group of people,' he said. I was introduced to the group one cold October morning.

We had just taken our seats in a colleague's office when a large man with black hair wearing a blue striped shirt and sports jacket appeared at the door. 'This is Liam,' Paul announced, looking enthusiastically at the newcomer. We exchanged greetings.

'I like your coat,' Liam whispered.

I felt pleased. I liked my orange coat. I wrapped it around me on cold days and felt cocooned from the biting wind.

After that initial meeting, I joined the group WhatsApp. Pretty soon I started noticing some strange messages appearing. 'I'm free today between 1.00 p.m. and 1.13 p.m. Anyone free for tea?' Paul's message said. *That's 13 minutes. Weirdly specific*, I thought to myself. Then again: 'I have twelve minutes free now if anyone is around.' *How odd.*

'How many clients do you have?' Paul would ask, before telling me that he had more clients and a busier schedule than I did. I found it strange. I was not aware of it being a competition.

'How much do you charge?' asked Paul, before telling me that he charged a good deal more than I did.

Paul talked a lot about his new car. I am not a car person, but I made encouraging noises.

Once, arriving at the office, I saw scribbled in large letters

I must not fail
I must not fail
I must not fail
I must not fail
I must not fail
I must not fail
I must not fail

on a sheet of paper placed on the desk. The writing was at a slight angle, the words were tight and cramped, and looked as though they were written in a frantic bid to silence an inner demon.

It was a strange moment. I wondered why he had left himself so open. I'm pretty sure now he never meant for me to see that.

Seeing my client exit the room, he would walk in abruptly, feigning apology. He started doing it more regularly.

It felt staged, like someone trying out a new technique. It felt intimidating. In his desperate bid not to fail, because it was a crippling, taunting feeling, he used me to quell the nagging voices in his head.

I let it go. Back then, I was someone who was easily pushed.

*

The supervision group continued through the winter and into the spring. I liked the group meetings, yet there was something amiss.

Liam didn't seem to have a lot to say. He nodded, he agreed, he made rather blunt, slightly coarse observations.

He didn't generally give new opinions but seemed to add on to another's opinion. He presented in a casual, likeable way, yet I was always surprised at how little he had to offer. He would grin a lot, giving away too much information about his clients with ease. I wondered whether he understood the concept of client confidentiality.

The comments he made stayed with me; I couldn't get them out of my mind. They jarred and scratched at something. It all felt rather unethical. Thanks to the lack of regulation around psychotherapy and counselling, however, officially it was all completely acceptable.

Whenever the two were in the room together, I noticed the way in which they communicated. A nod, a wink, wordless exchanges which puzzled me. They seemed to be part of the same person. They both seemed to be good at pretending, as if they were hollow structures, playing a game.

*

Months went by, spring arrived, and the days were getting longer. One Saturday night, somewhat at a loss as to what to do, I put a notice out on the supervision WhatsApp group:

'Anyone want to join me for a glass of wine?'

A few minutes later I received a response from Liam: 'I do.'

We met in a bar later that night. It didn't take long to realize that away from the supervision group, we enjoyed spending time together. I still didn't feel that we talked on the same level, but the night drew on all the same. I liked the attention, I liked the flirting. I liked feeling less lonely. The pub was warm and the seats were cozy. Couples were seated around the large, spacious room; there was a shelf full of whisky bottles, low lighting, and fires were lit on both sides of the room. It was a welcome break from a demanding week. Curved into each other, the conversation expanded to life outside of clients. Liam presented with a sort of naivete, his big arms stuffed into a tight shirt, chest hairs floating just above the level of the top button. He nodded his bulbous head and grinned. He seemed to be listening intently. He had something lodged in his teeth but I let it slide.

I let a lot of things slide that night.

The next day, he left my house early. I don't remember much of that night, but I know we did not sleep.

I felt oddly unnerved that morning and it was not a feeling I welcomed. I shoved the feeling out of the way and told myself it was nothing.

It was not nothing. It was everything.

But some things are only seen in the rear-view mirror, or years and years down the line.

THE WEEKEND AWAY

After a few weeks of nights out on the town, spending time getting to know one another, we decided to go away for the weekend together. Liam arrived mid-afternoon on a Friday, and we set off towards a picturesque West Cork town. The inside of his car was strewn with sweet wrappers, empty packets of chewing gum and paper bags. The seats and floor were dirty and there was a smell of slurry coming from somewhere.

I wondered how he could be arriving like this, but he appeared indifferent to the interior of his car. I had already felt apprehensive as he hooted the horn instead of knocking at the door; a vague feeling of unease passed over me.

It didn't improve. Seated at the small restaurant in the town, we had lunch and he suggested I foot the bill as he did not want to use his credit card. I was taken aback. We were in a relationship by now; surely it was probable he would use his credit card at some point?

I brushed off the feeling that it was deliberate. I paid the bill and we made our way down into the town, which was bursting at the seams with tourists, holidaymakers and residents who seemed, for the most part, happy to see their town filled to capacity.

All of the hotels were full, and we had not booked anywhere to stay. Another quiver of doubt passed through me but I shrugged it off. It was late, and we were running out of time to find a place to sleep for the night. The drive home was long and I was growing tired of finding the same answer at each place we visited:

Finally, a B & B owner took pity on us, and gave us a little room at the base of the staircase. I didn't mind; I was exhausted and fell asleep quickly.

My feeling of unease beside this bulk of a man had not improved. I had been trying to be on a date, but somewhere deep down there was a part of me saying loudly, persistently 'What are you doing?'

I ignored this voice, this part of me. It was inconvenient. I wanted to be here. 'I've met a nice man and I'm on a date. We're having a great time and there is no problem,' I said to myself. Inside, I was learning to wrestle with my gut feeling. I was developing ways to dampen it down. Over time, I would become pretty good at pushing my intuition away.

It's only later, when I meet Don Hennessy, when he looks at me with kind and intelligent eyes and says, 'Where has the real Suzanne gone?' that I understand what I was doing. What the cost of this battle with myself has been.

Back then, I was successfully ignoring all warning signs, for the most part. There were days when I felt like an object next to Liam, almost as if I was being examined for possible exploitation, yet I could not clearly understand it at that point. I had not understood the language of personal exploitation; how a master manipulator reels in his prey, one step at a time.

Liam asked me all about my life, my past, my hopes, my dreams, my daughter, what motivated me, what I valued.

I told him everything. It all spilled out. *Here's someone who really wanted to get to know me*, I thought.

I didn't know then that information was a weapon in his game plan, and that he would use it again and again.

A GAP IN THE FLOORBOARD

Liam greeted me at the front door to his farm house. 'Mind the gap,' he said, grinning, before pointing to a large hole just inside the foot of the front door. I peered down and was surprised to see a giant hole in the floorboard that I had to step over. It was hard to see anything below. An empty chasm at the entry point for the house. *Perfect for storing bodies*, I thought.

Having adjusted to the gloom inside the house, I started noticing the rooms running alongside the passageway. They were large and square and looked unused, dilapidated. The light fittings were old, and there was an odd smell of gas and mould emanating from the living room.

The kitchen was large, and at least that looked somewhat clean.

We exited the house from the back door of the kitchen and onto the large patch of lawn to the left of his house. A large wooden table and two chairs took centre stage, and we spent a pleasant afternoon drinking cider in the sun. The fields stretched out before us were vivid lime green, dotted with black and white cows, grazing in the dull heat.

It was peaceful until I heard a whining sound coming from a low-ceilinged green shed alongside the house.

His dogs were locked inside. I could hear them whimper. I was disappointed that he kept them there, but he seemed oblivious to their cries. I imagined them panting for air, trying desperately to get out. I heard them scrabbling and scratching at the door.

I asked him to let them out.

'They will run away,' he said. *With good reason*, I thought.

I drowned out the whimpering with more cider.

Eventually he let them out and the two large Labradors disappeared down the track towards the large stone wall surrounding the property.

By then the cider was taking hold of me. I forgot about the dogs, the hole in the floorboards, the smell and the strange feeling of the house. We were outside on a hot, sunny afternoon. I was enjoying the flirting, the way the black, thick hairs on his massive chest curved and fell. The sun and the cider and the chest hairs were blurring into one.

After a while, the sun started to sink and the effects of the cider wore off. I said goodbye and stepped over the gap in the floorboards once again, trying to peer surreptitiously into the depths hidden below.

As I walked to my car, the screech of crows could be heard from their perch up on the long, tent-like electricity lines above the house. It was a strange, unsettling cry, a mournful *Caw, caw, caw.*

Driving home, I couldn't stop thinking about his house. There was something strange about that house. It held secrets. I could feel it. There was an echo of a life lived in misery. The rooms had been left as if frozen in time. Only the kitchen seemed to have carried on living.

That night, I was woken by a feeling of dread in the pit of my stomach. My mind went over the day. *Nothing bad happened*, I thought. It was a good day. Then I remembered the gaping hole in the floorboard, the dogs trapped in the heated shed, and the strange *caw, caw, caw* of the crows.

I pushed the feeling of dread, the gaping floorboard, and the shed out of my mind and drifted back to sleep.

The faint sound of crows cawing invaded my dreamworld.

*

A few weeks went by and we decided to meet up again. The weather had turned cold.

Driving along a coastal route in East Cork, the cormorants looked tired and thin, standing amongst bits of kelp and wrack that lined the narrow inlet.

A harsh breeze strode through the air; bits of stone had been scattered far up the narrow road, stranded there after a full moon high tide.

The smell of salt and seaweed was pungent as we made our way around the inlet to the open water looking out towards Whitegate.

I was broke, as usual. I had been writing my thesis, working as a psychotherapist, and working part-time on a Sunday in a shop. It had all left me feeling rather stretched, and my bank account was empty.

I felt like a beer. I turned to Liam. 'Shall we go to the pub? Have a few beers?'

'Fine,' he said. The expression on his face was not so much a smile, as a smirk. 'But it's your turn to pay.'

'I'm broke,' I laughed, trying to make light of the situation, trying to find a way out of the corner I felt I was being steered into. His eyes narrowed and glittered. He had found something, a way in. He had come to know the shame I felt at being permanently broke, and he intended to use it as a way to push me into submission.

'It's your turn to pay,' he said, turning to me.

The car was stopped by the gray, dull water of the bay. I felt something slowly drag its nails over my stomach. It was a clawing, sick kind of feeling. I knew there was something happening here, but I could not fully articulate what it was. This was a power play. I felt like a toy he had in his possession. He was rounding in on me, but I did not understand it yet.

There was silence in the car. I was at a loss as to what to say. I felt stung. Arriving home, I was glad to be leaving his company.

Later that night, I remembered a conversation we had had a few weeks before. Liam had been boasting about how wealthy the counselling organization was that we both belonged to. 'They are loaded,' he said. 'Millions.'

I wondered why he would be concerned with what the organization made from its members. He often stated with pride how he had conned the system, charging the organization for miles travelled when he had not travelled them, how he had his eye on progressing up the ladder, targeting the pot of gold that was their bank account.

It all seemed a bit strange. Here was a man who owned a large amount of land, while I could barely pay rent, talking about the counselling organization, their millions, and how he could find his way into their pockets.

I didn't understand it then.

I understand it now.

A HOME IS NOT BRICKS AND MORTAR

Perhaps it was the feeling of loneliness that led me to accept his next invitation to meet up. Perhaps it was because I was starting to feel stuck. I was wary of Liam, but increasingly afraid to say no to his invitations.

We met at his farm a week after our drive around East Cork. By this point, we had been together about four months, and I found myself becoming confused and disturbed by the world I was being drawn into. He told me all about his marriage, why it broke down. 'She just stopped loving me,' he said.

He told me about the 'Exploring Sex' camps he had been on and what he had learned. He told me 'Exploring Sex' camps were good for the soul; he told me how he had undressed with all of the group members. How a woman had drawn over his body with a feather, and how it had made him ache with pleasure. His eyes gleamed as he talked. I could see it was a moment he dreamed about.

I found myself intrigued, fascinated by this other world. I wanted to know more, to know all the small details of what went on at the camps. I asked him to talk about it, to let me enter the world he was describing. He did so willingly.

He talked about the male participants. He told me how their big bodies and nakedness still lived in his mind. I could see a longing there. I could see that he was torn.

Naked men and naked women, all tantalizingly available. The camps were done on a farm nearby, and he remembered them vividly. I could see that the naked men occupied first position in his dreams.

Eventually the conversation moved away from his wife, the terrible things she had done to hurt him, the ways in which he had felt bereft and lonely when she left him.

He was painting a picture, unbeknownst to me. A victim's portrait.

It was all a lie, I found out years later. His wife did not leave him because she did not love him. His antics in the hot tub with a married man proved too much for her.

I would learn in time that he is an expert liar, a master manipulator, and strategist, and I was gradually reeled in, one step at a time. Having absorbed all of the information I so freely gave to him right from the start of our relationship, he was using it to draw me in.

He knew I wanted to help people. He knew I would always put another person's needs before my own. He knew this because I had told him. I was a perfect target.

I soaked it up at first. Despite all my misgivings, I wanted him to be the victim, I felt sorry for him. Here was a person I could help, and he would help me. We would both be less lonely. He told me the soundtrack to his divorce. How his choice of songs helped him with the pain of loss.

My subconscious mind, though, had other plans. Later that night, it came calling once more. I awoke with panic. I felt a fear pass over me that was becoming familiar. His words, even at that time, sounded false, made-up, not believable. He was acting the part of someone who has had heartbreak, acting first and foremost, as his shrivelled-up inner self constricted even further, unsure of what to do.

But I created another reason why that fear was there, how it had nothing to do with this man who is so good at being a victim and so brilliant at lying. I applied theories to the fear, and moved it to the side, denying its existence by rationalizing it.

I was becoming an expert at moving aside the only voice I should have been listening to.

Later in the conversation he asked, 'So what are your deal breakers?' I told him that above all else, I wanted a home that was comfortable and welcoming.

'I don't think I could ever live in your house,' I told him, in my blunt, South African way.

He did not seem particularly affected by the remark. 'A home is just bricks and mortar,' he said.

It was a contract being drawn up. A sizing-up of what I would be wanting. It sounded like an invitation, though nothing further was said.

The comment stayed with me. I thought of my grandmother's house.

Jacaranda House. The long, red brick house is decorated with lush gardens. There are family members dotted all over the lawn. Some are laughing, some are talking. My cousins are playing football, arguing over the last point.

My aunt is tending the rose bed, her favourite place in the garden. My grandmother is seated on the floral red and white garden chair in the shade, out of the baking South African sun. Deep pink bougainvillea stride up the red bricked wall that divides the front of the garden from the kitchen entrance. There is a feeling of immense peace in this place. This home is a place where family and friends gather. This home is where family members make food and eat together. This home has a soul.

A home is *not* just bricks and mortar.

AN ENDING OF SORTS

The summer was unusually warm and sunny that year. We met every week, sometimes for a drink at a local bar, sometimes for a walk or a visit to his farm.

Entering the gates to the farm, I felt the rest of the world disappear. Driving up the small, narrow lane leading to the cow sheds and the large stack of animal food for the winter piled high up, I felt time slowing down. Sometimes it was a welcome change from the busyness of the week, sometimes it was too quiet, the only sound coming from the crows on the lawn.

We talked about what we wanted, what we yearned for.

'I feel lonely,' he said. 'I struggle with loneliness on the farm and I hate coming in late after seeing my clients and into a dark, cold house.'

I believed him. I could see that living by himself on a large farm would be lonely. I was drawn into that isolation and felt that I could be someone he could talk to, someone he could lean on, someone he could feel less lonely with and that I could feel less lonely too.

There were times that conversations like these would settle the restless, incessant feeling of doubt that kept interrupting this potential for a future, that imagined life. I could see myself baking things, planting flower beds. It was a lovely picture in my mind's eye.

But the doubt would not leave. The fear did not pass. I found that with each drive up to the farm, I was starting to feel more isolated. The visits were starting to intrude on my normal life and I was starting to feel more and more cut-off. Each time we would meet up, every time I would go to his farm, I could not settle, the feeling of isolation weighing heavily on me. It was like a cage was descending over me, separating me from my normal world, fixedly, determinedly.

On the slow drive home, a feeling of relief would wash over me. I would walk into my small kitchen in the small estate next to the community hall bustling with various activities, and relish the fact that I was home again, safe.

Often I would awake at night, a sharp, searing feeling of fear slicing through my chest. It was becoming untenable, this feeling of fear always surfacing after our meetings.

Five months into our relationship, at the end of August 2016, I knew I had to end it. The constant put-downs and throwaway cruelties, feeling fearful and isolated in his company, were finally getting to be too much. I resented the mind-numbingly repetitive conversations, the constant preoccupation with money that he had, the way he seemed fixated on me, obsessive, like I was something he wanted to own.

On a Saturday afternoon, walking together along the narrow road that wound its way to Blackrock Castle, I gently made it known I wanted to end the relationship.

It was a warm day. The smell of flowers drifted over the garden walls. Bees ambled back and forth over the narrow street, uninterrupted in their quest. The clear skies seemed to be saying that this was right. This was for the best. This was the way forward. He seemed to take it well, he nodded his head, we agreed we would be friends and we parted company. The word that comes to mind is a civil goodbye.

I remember arriving home, and the sense of relief accompanying me.

I'm glad that's over, I thought to myself.

It was far from over.

STALKING

Later that year, I started receiving messages from Liam to meet up 'for a pint'. Not frequently, but enough to make me feel unsettled.

Each time the invitation arrived, I felt frozen, like a deer in the headlights. I would stare fixedly at the message, my eyes unblinking.

Not knowing how to respond, I would remain polite and say no.

The messages persisted.

Sometimes I would say yes.

The warning bells persisted.

Occasionally, I would arrive home, and turning into my street I would see his car, parked facing the entrance to my estate. *That's odd*, I thought to myself. *That's a strange place to park.*

A few minutes later I'd receive a message. 'I'm just in the area, are you free?' it would say, or words to that effect.

I felt that familiar feeling of unease. *How could he just happen to be parked outside my estate?* I wondered.

This happened frequently. Sometimes I would see his car and not get a text.

Sometimes I would receive a text without seeing his car. It almost always read the same way: 'Feel like a pint?'

The messages persisted.

There was a pattern developing. Weeks would go by and he would be silent, then out of the blue, a message again. Again, I would see his car, the familiar registration number, the familiar twisting, sweaty nausea in the pit of my stomach.

I was being followed.

At the time, I did not entertain the idea that this was stalking. At the time, I had no language to describe what it was, only that it was obsessive, intrusive, and disturbing. I was under surveillance.

I did not put the word 'stalking' to the behaviour. Stalking, to my old self, was something that happened to other people in movies. Stalking was something you would read about or hear about. It happened over there, to other people, famous people, people in other countries.

Stalking did not happen in Ireland.

Stalking was a word that was never used in conversation. It was a dark, hidden act that was invisible and terrifying. I had never come across someone who had been stalked. In truth, I had come across many people who had been stalked, but the terminology in Ireland was – and still is – harassment.

The language we use to describe behaviour is powerful. If a behaviour is not named with the correct language, then we do not understand it completely, and we do not understand the intent behind it.

I did not understand, then, that this was stalking.

So I dismissed my fears, and at times, agreed to meet up. I felt permanently trapped between a fear of accepting the invitation, and an even greater fear of saying no. I felt that, if I said no, he would turn on me.

I was right.

A WALK

Despite breaking up with Liam, and wanting to sever ties with him, our paths kept crossing. Even if I said no to a suggestion for meeting up, we were both part of the same counselling and psychotherapy organization. We were in the same profession. We were in contact with the same people, in the same East Cork counselling circle. We would meet at a conference or talks held by the organization. I felt that I had to keep civil, professional. He mistook this for encouragement.

I would often walk into the large hotel conference rooms where the meetings took place, hoping that this time he would not be there, but he always was. I remained polite, he remained insistent, and the messages persisted.

My two-year college course was coming to an end, and in October 2017 it was graduation day. He knew I was graduating; I had told him. He suggested we meet for a walk after graduation. I reluctantly agreed.

Graduation day was a festive celebration. Walking on stage, the man handing out the certificates stopped me and congratulated me on my results. I was beaming as I walked off the stage. It was a good moment. The graduation class was jubilant. It had been a long two years and we were all glad to be crossing the finishing line. After the graduation ceremony, there were photographs taken, cheers and laughter, and a knowledge that we would always be connected in some way because of this achievement.

The next day, Liam and I met for a walk near the large community hall, and started along the winding, narrow road that led from the village into the surrounding countryside. He talked a lot about himself initially, and then the conversation moved to inanities. I remembered what it was like to be in his company. Even still, knowing what I know of him, his incessant self-absorption, I was taken aback that he had not mentioned my graduation. We continued our walk. About halfway back to the community hall near my house, he asked nonchalantly, 'So, what did you get up to yesterday?'

A wave of nausea passed over me.

His conversation felt like a staged approach to a life by someone whose intentions are always to crush anything with a light inside. After the high note of yesterday, the cheers and the group photographs, I was aware he had decided to intrude on the joy that I was experiencing, to flatten me down.

It felt like a game. He was toying with me.

I told him I had graduated.

'Oh yes', he said, pretending again. 'What mark did you get?'

He knew full well what my mark was. I told him anyway.

'Oh right,' he said, as if he'd forgotten. 'Didn't five other people also get a First?' he asked, sounding dismissive. He didn't want me to do well. Inwardly, he was baring his teeth.

By that stage, I was ready to go home. I had grown tired of playing this game.

We walked on, but inside, I had left. I was home and sitting in my living room, listening to Miles Davis playing *In A Silent Way*. I had a glass of wine in front of me, and the sound of the outside world was drowned out by the hauntingly beautiful lines of the trumpet. I often used this survival tactic with Liam. It was a way to escape.

The rest of the conversation was a blur. I had gone somewhere else because I had remembered why I never wanted to be with him.

A WALK

When Liam left the house that day, I saw something that I registered as odd, but dismissed it quickly. He gave my neighbour the strangest look when he left. He stood at the front door, turned to the house on the right, and grinned at the neighbour, someone I never really spoke to, nodding his head. It seemed conspiratorial. There was a secret being shared, but I didn't understand it then. To my knowledge, the two had never met before. It was a look that came back to haunt me.

After the walk, our meetups became less and less frequent. I was growing tired of the same conversations, the same dull responses, the same feeling of being diminished and trapped.

Even though I was afraid of saying no, I began to say no to his messages more often, and hoped he would leave me alone.

He didn't leave me alone.

THE GRIEVANCE

After the walk, the messages persisted.

I began to attend the counselling meetings and conferences less frequently as a way of avoiding him. Liam had decided that, in keeping with his strategy to gain access to the funds of the organization, he would become more and more involved in the running of one of the committees. And the more he became involved in the running of the committee, the less I attended the meetings.

At the beginning of 2018 I moved from the office on the main street and joined a thriving psychotherapy practice nearby. I was happy in my new position there. It was an established practice and the team worked well together. I enjoyed the drive to work, the busyness of the day and the slow drive home. I enjoyed my work with clients and meeting the team for lunch or a quick cup of tea. The conversations about my field, liaising with doctors and psychiatrists, and the ongoing attention to keeping the practice running smoothly and professionally gave me a sense of immense satisfaction and fulfilment.

The practice was housed in a beautiful old building with a great sense of community. Finally, I was working with people who were really committed to providing a great service and forming alliances, and who were invested in something greater than themselves. As the year progressed, I started to forget all about Liam and the way in which our paths had crossed. I had taken time away from relationships and was enjoying the pace of life.

One cold October evening in 2019, I received a message. 'Fancy a pint…?'

I froze. That familiar feeling of being stuck washed over me like a wave. I stared at the message.

I put the phone away and went on with my day. After a few hours of feeling uneasy a sense of disquiet roamed the inside of my mind. I could not settle. By early evening, I was rattled. I was afraid of him. I was afraid of what he could do to my professional world.

A part of me knew, even then, that he had the ability to seriously impact my new professional life. I valued it too much; I wanted to keep it.

So I said yes.

We made our way to our favourite bar, a brightly lit venue in the town. It was comfortably busy and I felt the background chatter soothe my tired head, dousing the ever-present feeling of disquiet in his company. We chatted on and on; I cannot remember what we spoke about. Eventually it was time to go home. Walking me to my car, parked conveniently next to his, he stroked my coat.

'This is a lovely coat,' he said, sounding vaguely menacing.

I think it was the alcohol that led me into his car; that, or the need to feel warm. After a while, he pushed his massive frame onto mine, and I realized that I needed to call an end to the evening.

'Get off me,' I said.

The air froze. He lumbered off my side of the car, and seemed to be paused, deep in thought. Something had changed. A feeling of violence entered the space between us. He stared, unblinking, out of the front window. I could see how his expression changed. It was an expression of rage. He gave me a look I had not seen before, his eyes cold and empty. His mouth, usually a veneer of pseudo-friendliness, was now set in a tense line, his jaw locked and stiff. He was seething with rage, a deep, vengeful rage that had been lying just under the surface, waiting to get out.

He said nothing.

A loud, ringing warning bell was sounding in my ears.

Hurriedly leaving the car, muttering something to ease the silence that had enveloped us both, I drove off.

I could not sleep that night.

*

That was the beginning. That was the moment that everything changed. The veneer had gone, the politeness had gone, his rage at being rejected was clear.

Up till that point, he had managed the polite rejection I had offered with a polite, fake friendliness. He had persisted because he felt in time I would cave. I would give in. He would eventually have me.

Now, I had rejected his sexual advances. I had rejected *him* outright. This was not a polite breakup. This was not a walk in the country. This was me saying no to something he felt entitled to. This was something that he felt he was always going to get in the end, that his persistence was eventually going to pay off. That I was his, mind and body.

And I didn't do it politely. I said, 'Get off me.' I had drawn a hard line, on my terms, and he could not accept it.

Years later, I think of that moment still. The way in which I wrestled with myself, the way in which I had chosen to meet him that evening, even though I was afraid. The way I had felt so trapped.

I could not sleep that night. The fear had returned and multiplied.

After that, there were no more messages.

No more invitations were issued. A resounding silence seemed to follow.

And while the messages and invitations abruptly stopped, something even more sinister started.

*

The next day I woke to find my front garden had been littered with rubbish. I presumed the wind had blown it there, since there was only a low wall separating my house from the road. I picked it up and forgot about it. The next morning, stepping out on a brisk October day, I noticed still more rubbish in my garden. This time it was a few bags of dog excrement, wrapped in a plastic bag.

I picked it up with a sigh of disgust.

The next day, more rubbish. I also came home to find my sliding door ajar. *Did I leave it open?* I wondered.

Leaving later that day I made sure the door was closed properly, the garden cleared of new rubbish.

When I returned an hour later, the door was once again open, and more rubbish had been strewn on the lawn.

Becoming annoyed, I closed the door, and, picking up the rubbish, I noticed my neighbour – a small, scrawny man in his thirties; the neighbour that Liam had looked at in such a conspiratorial way – standing staring at me, a slight smirk at the corner of his mouth.

That's odd, I thought. I had never before noticed that neighbour looking at me, studying me so closely. I felt unnerved. Why was he smirking at me?

The garden rubbish and opened door continued, despite my numerous attempts to lock the sliding door.

That evening, I started to notice a few cars passing me repeatedly while I was out walking.

There were five vehicles I could make out that circulated around me. I felt confused. What on earth was happening?

I started to notice the same cars each time I went on my daily walks.

I changed the time of day when I went walking,

I changed my route.

Yet they always seemed to be there, driving past again and again while I went walking. The confusion progressed to alarm. *Why would someone follow me on my walks?* I wondered. It was a country lane, it didn't lead anywhere except to more country lanes. As my route was a loop, it would mean that it was being done on purpose, cars looping round and round, encircling me.

From that day onwards, I felt a slow circle being drawn around me. Not too closely to begin with. At the start, everything appeared rather random, despite the looping round and round and round.

Despite the garden refuse being dumped again and again and again.

Despite the sliding door opened, shut, Opened, shut, opened.

This series of apparently random attacks were the start of something that would continue for years to come, and still continues. A slow and gradual web being formed which was sticky, intricate, intangible. Back and forth and back and forth they wove the web increasingly tighter around me.

I felt a strong sense of unease. I had started noticing my neighbour more and more and he was watching me. I would step outside in the early morning. Tending to the flower beds, I heard the sound of a door opening. There was my neighbour. He would stand at his door, staring at me.

'Doing a bit of weeding are we?' he mumbled.

I ignored his comment and kept working in the garden.

At night, I would hear a tap, tap, tap on my window.

I opened the window and saw nothing which would make this sound.

A while later, drifting off to sleep, I would hear the tapping again. After a while it became louder, more persistent.

It sounded like it was coming from the upstairs bathroom wall. I started to think I was hearing things. How could it be coming from the bathroom wall? The persistent tapping and banging at night was starting to make me feel tired and jumpy during the day. My concentration was starting to falter. I decided to place a security camera on the back window.

One day, putting away the garden tools in the narrow passageway between the two adjoining houses, I looked up. And then it occurred to me: the bathroom wall was easy to bang on from here. All you needed was a long pole.

There was a long pole balanced against the wall, conveniently placed for the neighbour to access. That was how he managed it.

My question still remained: *why* had his behaviour changed towards me? I remembered the conspiratorial look Liam and my neighbour had given each other. That had been six months ago, but it felt like yesterday.

A family member arrived for the month of December that year, and the weaving stopped. The following stopped. The garden refuse stopped and the sliding door remained closed.

Silence.

Once the family member left, the refuse started again.

The sliding door, open, shut, open, shut.

The following in the car, round and round and round.

I started walking in a group. It continued, regardless.

I voiced my fear tentatively to friends, not really being sure of how to say what it was that I was experiencing. They voiced their concern.

The nightly tap, tap, tap on the bathroom wall began again. After a while, the noise became softer, less obvious, but just as effective. I awoke each night, falling back into fitful shards of sleep. The next day, I was slower, more distracted, and less able to function.

This continued, on and on and on. One morning I woke to the sound of snoring. It seemed to be coming from the attic directly above me.

That's impossible, I thought. *How on earth would someone get up there to sleep?* Later that day, I climbed up the ladder and into the attic.

An opened packet of crisps and an empty can had been left in the area just above my bedroom.

A CHANGE IN THE AIR

On February 15th 2020 the AGM of the counselling organization we belonged to took place in a nearby hotel. Filled with apprehension about meeting Liam again, I found my way to the large conference room. I saw him out of the corner of my eye as I took a seat next to a colleague. His eyes were following me around the room. The familiar tight, sweaty knot had formed in the pit of my stomach. That familiar feeling of discomfort around him, that unsettled feeling I have been so good at silencing, had now found a voice inside me, and it was speaking loudly and clearly: *Run!*

I didn't run, of course. I made myself sit down, and tried to listen to what was being said.

Midway through the conference, we were given a half-hour tea break. I made for the tea table and noticed him standing there. I decided to start a conversation, mostly to test the waters. 'Hello,' I said. 'It's a nice turnout for the day.'

He stared at me coldly, his eyes blank and empty. It was a strange kind of look, the same look he had given me that night in the car, full of rage just beneath a veneer. It was a look meant to crush me. I felt its aim and I felt the force of the blow. We exchanged a thin layer of pleasantries, before moving to different corners of the room. Filling my cup of tea from the large urn before me, I tried to settle the impulse to leave the room.

His friend Paul – the one who had scribbled 'I cannot fail' on an A4 sheet of paper back when I first started sharing office space – moved, serpent-like, towards me.

'Hello, Suzanne,' he whispered with malice in his voice. He seemed to know something I didn't. It felt like he was watching my every move. After a brief chat, I made my way out of his grasp, intending to avoid his slippery presence for the rest of the day. It was not to be. He seemed to follow me everywhere I went. Coming back from a coffee break, I noticed he was standing very close to my handbag and seemed to be placing something in it. I dismissed the thought outright. What on earth would he want in my handbag? I looked through the bag. There was nothing amiss. Was it part of the game they were playing – toying with me, playing with my mind?

Paul seemed to be wearing the same smirk. The same expression. The same malice exuding from his cheap cologne and worn, faded jeans.

I was sure Paul was colluding with Liam. Collusion is a powerful weapon. Collusion is the means by which people excuse themselves from saying that they participated in acts of violence. Onlookers, participants, can argue that they were merely watching. I had tested the waters, and found sharks beneath the surface. Round and round they were circling, keeping me under close watch, waiting for the right time to strike.

I was deeply afraid.

EXPLOSION

Early in March 2020, rumours of a global pandemic spreading across the world grabbed the headlines and by the end of March the world had grown quiet. Restrictions were set across the world for travel, for general movement to and from work, and a two-kilometre limit had been placed on all households across Ireland.

As freedom of movement and social interaction came to an abrupt halt, my own situation was getting even weirder.

I started to notice that while walking the two-kilometre loop again and again the number of cars following me had increased. Dramatically.

Now it seemed as if there were ten cars, fifteen, twenty; round and round and round.

This can't be happening, I would say to myself. *This is just in your head. You're imagining things.*

I argued my way out of my own instinctive knowledge, just as I had argued my way out of feeling afraid around Liam. It lasted for a while. There were only five cars following me; it was nothing, just people who were bored. *But why would they keep doing this?* I wondered. *Who is paying their diesel bill?*

I sought out the narrowest of roads, and went walking early in the morning or late in the evening. It didn't seem to matter how hard I tried to avoid being followed, it happened regardless.

One evening, arriving home from work, I noticed that my back door lock had been broken.

The door stood ajar and there were fish oil capsules sprinkled liberally over the landing upstairs. I noticed some of my photographs had been taken out of their frames and placed on my tabletop.

It was chilling to imagine someone in my house. Someone browsing through my cupboards, taking out vitamins and pouring them over the carpet. It was even more chilling to think of someone taking photographs out of their frames, and placing them alongside the frames. It seemed so sinister. It seemed so purposeful.

Why the fish oil capsules? Nothing was taken; it was more like someone was playing a game with my mind. Toying with me, constantly putting things in my way to see what my response would be.

I thought of someone striding around my house in daylight, going through each drawer, choosing which things to disturb and which to leave untouched. Had he decided to do this or was he being directed?

It was also during a time when anyone entering another person's house added an additional fear: the fear of contracting COVID-19. There were reports of people dying in hospitals with nobody at their side for fear of contamination. *Could I contract Covid from this person?*

I called the locksmith and a friendly man arrived soon after. 'If someone really wants to get into your house, they will,' he said.

Over the next few years, these words ricocheted around my head. How true they have proven to be.

A policeman arrived, masked and friendly. I explained how my house had been broken into, the back door lock broken. He could see that only one person could have accessed my back garden, which leads to the back door: my neighbour.

'He's a known criminal and bully,' he said. I could believe it. He said he would have a few words with him, and leaving the house, seemed to pause at the front door. He looked at the neighbour's house, and left.

I wondered why he hadn't taken a statement from me. Perhaps because nothing had been taken. Nothing had been broken, apart from the back door lock. But I felt uneasy at the thought that nothing had been written down. Now I had no record of the incident.

I closed the door and went upstairs, feeling unsettled and unprotected.

I started to lock windows and doors with ever-increasing vigilance. I bought a security camera and stuck it on the front door.

Now I'll be left in peace, I thought.

I could not have been more mistaken.

CAT AND MOUSE

Lockdown was in full swing and we were all two metres apart, waiting patiently to walk around the supermarket. We were loading up food for the week, so as to minimize contact with others. Masked and on-edge, people avoided each other. I was on edge for a different reason. I was becoming more and more concerned with what was happening at home: being followed on my walks endlessly. I started to suspect that this trend was becoming a more widespread activity, involving a lot more people.

As I waited in the queue, or walked around the shop, I started to notice something very strange: People seemed to be looking at their phones, and then looking pointedly at me, smirking slightly, and then back at their phones. All non-verbal communication.

It was an extension of the game, the experiment. An extension of what had happened up till that point. Cat and mouse, predator and prey. Toying with me, constantly trying to unravel me. I was under surveillance continuously.

What was being communicated was not friendly. Friendly communication is a smile, a hello, a friendly acknowledgement, a warm feeling. This was different. This communication was intrusive and sinister.

This happened on more than one occasion; this happened every day, all the time, when people were on foot and passed me by. I saw them checking their phones, then at me, and then back again. It was unnerving. It was disturbing. *Surely they can't be looking at me, following me, watching me,* I thought. *Surely they're just checking shopping lists, checking to see who was messaging them, looking at something on YouTube. Surely, I thought, the way that they're pointedly looking at me and then their phones is purely coincidental.*

It persisted.

One month of this behaviour became two months, then three and four months. The summer rolled on and it kept on happening, regardless of where I would go and who I was with. I was starting to feel very alone. The strangeness of this was matched by the ongoing troubles with the neighbour, and the combined effect was exhausting. I tried surreptitiously to see what people were looking at on their phones but it was hard to do with the two-metre gap that was enforced due to Covid.

After a while it started happening on the small country roads where I walked to avoid cars. The demographic was mostly male, mostly between the age of 20 to late fifties. Over time, this changed, and more women were used. Their methodology was simple. On approach, they had their phones in hand, extended and raised, looking at them. Then they looked at me, back at their phones, and then back at me.

It was done as a way to taunt me, to indicate that I was being watched and my movements were being tracked everywhere I went. It was done in an obvious way, to signal to me and the others following me that I was the target. When they approached me, there was a slight smirk at the edges of their mouths. They seemed buoyed-up by life, they seemed in control and enthusiastic in their mission. They seemed to know something I didn't. This pattern was repeated by all who participated.

That summer I was walking along a deserted narrow road when a thin, medium-height man walked towards me, looking at his phone, then at me, and then back at his phone, that same slight smirk appearing at the corner of his mouth. I snapped and strode up to him, angered by the continued invasion into my life. I knew he was one of the participants: the same actions, the same look, the same feeling in the pit of my stomach, all told me he was one of them.

'Are you part of the game?' I asked.

He shuffled forward, dropping his eye contact with me. The smirk had disappeared.

'What platform are you using?' I asked. He slowed his pace. He was becoming uneasy, I could see it. 'Is it WhatsApp, is it Snapchat, is it Discord?'

He stopped. 'We don't use any platforms,' he said.

Sensing that he had been caught out, he began to pick up speed, veering towards the far left of the narrow road.

'How much are you being paid?' I threw one last question his way, but he was now walking at pace, and soon he had rounded the bend and was gone.

I stood there for a while. It was a strange response. It indicated knowing something. His comment stayed with me. I knew he had given something away.

I wanted to know more. I needed to know more. What information about me was being viewed as they passed me by, relishing in the fact that they were part of a big cat and mouse game?

I was confused and alarmed. At that stage, although I knew who was behind these stalking behaviours, I had not yet received confirmation. I had no idea of the much bigger picture. I had not met Don Hennessy or Liam's brothers (for I discovered later that he had two older brothers who were also involved.)

All I knew then was that something big was happening. Something that required careful orchestration, planning, time, and money. I was overwhelmed by what I was being subjected to, and at a loss as to what words to put on my experience.

*

CAT AND MOUSE

In May 2020, when lockdown was being strictly enforced, I decided to test my theory about being followed by a large group of unknown people. I drove to a small, secluded beach nearby, to see if anyone followed me there.

It was a cold, windy day. Clouds scurried across the sky, billowing out before disappearing forever, drops in the atmosphere.

Arriving at the beach, I ventured down the narrow laneway that led to a small parking lot and maneuvered the car so that I faced the entrance to the laneway. I pulled up the handbrake and turned off the ignition.

The beach was completely empty. No cars were in sight, and no walkers roamed along the beachfront. My shoulders were rigid with tension. I peered anxiously towards the narrow lane leading onto the beach, waiting.

After about three minutes, a black car with no front number plate came into view. As the car passed by, it stopped and the driver paused, looking directly at me.

I felt a small sharp spear of fear. I wondered whether to drive away, but I was becoming tired of being on the move, relentlessly pursued and toyed with. A rabbit down the rabbit hole, dogs baying at the scent. I was growing tired of running. I stayed in my car, and the other car turned on the narrow patch of grass and parked directly behind me.

Eventually a man got out of the car and walked to the beach, retrieving his phone and pointing it at me. He seemed to say, *We have located you. You are our prey and we will find you, wherever you are.* I stared in the rearview mirror and the man with the phone stared back. Amidst the fear – and the bewilderment as to what this game was for, what its motives were – arrived another feeling. A feeling of anger. My jaw was clenched, my teeth were grinding against each other.

I rested my hand on the car door, tempted to open it and make my way over. I stopped and considered.

I had come across two types of participants: coerced and eager. The coerced participant I'd met previously had seemed drawn and afraid. Her eyes had refused to meet mine; she had seemed bewildered and unwilling, a reluctant and fearful participant.

The man in the black car was a willing actor who had been given a script. *Do this, and then do this, and look like this,* the script said. *Then do this and say nothing to her. Then drive away.*

It was like they'd all been given strict instructions on what to say or do. Imagine the time it took for these scripts to be written. The level of intent it took to drive someone to put this amount of energy into something so bizarre.

Did anyone change it, improvise? Was it all pre-planned? The mind boggled. Why would someone sign up for this; why fulfil another's desire for revenge?

There was only one answer: money.

I imagined there being a cash reward for participants. An envelope in the post, perhaps. However it was exchanged, it was a transaction. *You do this, we give you that.* The higher the risk taken, the bigger reward. The increased feel-good factor. The new pair of shoes. The new shirt. The new car. Some were easy to buy, others required a more generous incentive.

There were at least five people on a monthly retainer, their small black cars a regular feature on my daily travels. I wondered how all this money was being accumulated. Drugs?

Probably. It was all so strange.

Deciding against talking to the man, I stayed put and played some music on my phone. Perhaps the idea was to get me to leave this secluded beach and go back home. I wasn't falling for that; instead I tried to focus on the landscape, the sea, the smells in the air, trying to block out the rising anxiety.

In a recent report on stalking, a survey took note of the ways in which victims of stalkers try to escape the stalker. The survey described how victims of stalking move house, move country, change phone numbers, change cars, change the locks on their doors, change their identity.

I was only grasping at the edges of just how terrifying this was, but in time, I would come to consider all of the above as ways to break free.

THE MUSIC GROUP

By June that year, I was feeling worn out. The break-ins continued, as did the lack of support from the police. There were still strict Covid regulations, and people were just at the point of being able to meet outdoors; distanced, of course, but at least it was something to break the isolation of lockdown. I discovered via a friend that a music group was beginning to meet up regularly in someone's garden. The idea sounded wonderful. I contacted the organizer of the group and was warmly welcomed the following Wednesday.

It was summer, and we sat outdoors, distanced but together at least. I felt uplifted, even before the music began.

The music group was composed of a large number of musicians, most of whom had been playing traditional Irish music for a lot longer than I had.

Seated on the benches or chairs arranged in a circle, I was nervous about taking part in the evening's session. The friendly banter and laughter put my mind at ease to some degree, and we gradually gave way to making a start on the evening's tunes. We started with 'The Kerry Polka', and moved from there. Being there was a magical experience. The tunes buried themselves in my skin and formed a warm lining that spread through my body. I didn't notice time passing; I was focussed entirely on keeping up with the steady pace, and hoping nobody noticed when I played the wrong chord.

My comfort zone, strictly speaking, is playing folk and jazz. Irish tunes are still somewhat of a mystery to me.

We sang songs, we played tunes, and took a break halfway through the night.

The meetings continued for months and are still taking place. Every Wednesday, I could sit with this group, and forget that I was a target in a vicious game. I could feel like I had a community of friends, and that we did not talk about all the things that were going wrong in the world. This was a time to connect in a different way. In a profoundly healing way. I am sure that without this group, I would have struggled even more.

Later that autumn, when the nights started to become colder, we moved our music sessions to a dilapidated old wooden barn. It was a wonderful setting that allowed us to continue playing despite the restrictions still in place as the Irish winter drew near. We would take up our seats on bales of hay and old chairs before beginning the night's music.

An assortment of bottles of wine and beer stood on the wooden table. Candles dotted around the room provided the lighting. In there, I forgot about the violence of being stalked, of people trying to intimidate me, and endlessly following me. There, I could drop the mask, fold into the music, and fill up again after a draining week.

For this brief time, I felt safe. The music gently escorted my whirring mind to a still place, a place where I was connected. I didn't have the proper words yet to describe what was happening to me and because of that I felt isolated. With this music, the isolation was broken, and I was part of something bigger than just me and my guitar. I didn't speak of what was happening to me, of being observed day and night. Here I was invisible in the best possible way. I was part of something moving, expanding, contracting, indivisible from the rest.

After the break, we returned to our seats, and a fiddle player started a slow air. These were my favourite tunes. I loved their slow rise and fall, the melody line seeming to float between rhythms.

It was a magical time.

Later on, I was to find another music group, having moved away from the countryside in an attempt an escape from being stalked.

The new music group also met on Wednesdays.

And so my relationship with Wednesday evenings and music was to continue, and still continues to this day.

It has been one of the things that has saved me.

NEW LEVELS OF BIZARRE

By mid-July 2020, things at home had reached new levels of menace and intimidation.

I often came home to find my front door open. My car was frequently open when I came to it each morning; people sped up and down the roads when I went on long walks, which became increasingly shorter as time went by. I was jumpy and nervous, unable to feel safe and secure anywhere.

I would walk home to find cars parked outside my house, which sped up and left once I arrived home. There seemed to be a constant noise, continual movement, never still. And I was growing increasingly frustrated with the lack of response from the police.

One morning, around 5.00 a.m., I woke to the familiar banging on my bathroom wall. Bang bang, bang bang. It was my neighbour. The small, yellow-teeth and shaven-head neighbour. I had now been tormented by being woken up by the banging for nearly six months. I felt frayed and thin at the edges, sleep-deprived and rattled.

I went into the small, narrow storage space between the two adjoining houses, and grabbed the long pole, now lying flat on the ground. Rage and frustration exploded from within me and I started banging loudly and incessantly on the walls. A few minutes went by.

All of a sudden, the door from the neighbour's house flew open and he stormed into the narrow passageway.

'What the fuck are you doing?' he yelled, his yellow teeth bared. 'Stop banging! Stop banging, stop banging!' He came at me and shoved me hard against the door. 'I'll kill you! I'll kill you, I'll kill you!' he shouted, over and over and over. I leaned hard into the wooden door and managed to open it enough to get out, slamming it shut and locking it as quickly as I could.

I was breathing heavily, adrenaline rushing into every vein in my body, full of fear, full of rage.

Later on that morning, once I had composed myself to some degree, I paid a visit to the police station. The same police officer came to the house and asked me what had happened. I explained and he went away, notebook in hand but nothing written down. There were no statements taken; my neighbour was not questioned.

A while later, I once more phoned the police station to find out what had been done. This is the answer I received: my landlord had been questioned about the incident and that, as he did not witness the event at 5.00 a.m., he could not verify what happened. He also did not want to get involved.

I was stunned. 'This person is making my life very difficult,' I said. 'He wakes me up every night, he has shoved me against the door and yelled "I'll kill you!" at me. What does my landlord have to do with it? I am saying that I have been *assaulted* and *threatened*.'

Nothing was done about this event. No statements were ever taken. I could not get an answer from the police.

I found myself wondering, *Where in the legal system does it state that a landlord's perspective on an event he/she did not witness hold more weight than the person actually being assaulted?*

I was deeply confused and dazed by the strangeness of it all. Why was it so hard to understand? I was being tormented. Why was nobody listening?

NEW LEVELS OF BIZARRE

I was slowly being eroded, like a cliff that started to crumble, one small rock at a time. The feeling of things being broken within, wearing away, little by little. Every time I approached the police, I could hear my voice getting softer and softer, drowned out by the opinion of others.

THE PRIVATE DETECTIVE

After the experience with my neighbour, I decided to seek outside help.

I googled *private detectives in Cork*. After a brief conversion with someone who seemed to fit that description, we arranged that he come to the house later that week to assess the problem.

The private detective walked firmly into the house. Scanning the house en route into the kitchen, he sat down and we began to talk.

'I'm not sure if I completely get the picture,' he said after a while .

Great, I thought. *Just what I need.*

He offered to do a read of the house and car to check if there were any hidden cameras or listening devices planted anywhere. Striding out of the house, he abruptly returned with a small black case and proudly extracted a device that would, he asserted, find all such devices so he could remove them accordingly. Shuffling round each room, in a random sort of way, half-heartedly waving the device at the corners of the room, he was clearly disinterested in what I was saying and trying to communicate to him.

Then he announced proudly 'All clear. What you need,' he said, his eyes roaming up and down the length of my body, 'is a good ride.' I stared at him blankly, unable to hear what it was that he had said. He repeated himself, assuming that I had not heard him the first time. 'What you need now, girl, is a good ride. Yes,' he ventured further, 'you just need someone to come over three times a week and this problem will go away.'

I was too stunned to speak.

'If you don't have anyone at the moment,' he continued, 'I'd be more than willing to, um, do the job for you.'

I looked at his fat face, his top lip trembling with anticipation. His belt had come loose and his shoes were worn and scuffed.

I'm scared, I felt like saying. *I'm afraid. I need protection. I'm trying to make my world safe again, but you're making things even worse. I feel even more unsafe now.*

I could feel a deep wail starting to emerge but shut it up firmly. *No room for crying now,* I said to myself. Wanting him out of my house as fast as possible, I pretended to be grateful for his help.

'Really, you've been very helpful,' I lied. 'I'll give you a call if anything else comes up.'

He heaved himself into his car, the front wheels bowing as he set himself into position. Giving me a sly smile, he drove away.

I returned to the house and sat down. That familiar feeling: defeat. A deep, empty void threatened to swallow me up. I felt deflated. Crushed. My world was falling apart. My sense of what was safe and who was safe was falling apart.

I found it hard to move for the rest of the day. The dark, sweaty nausea that welled up inside me refused to leave.

It lingered for that day, and the next, and it was only when I went to my familiar yoga class in the GAA hall in the local village that it started to ebb away.

At the end of the class, the yoga teacher, with a warm smile on her face, wrapped my feet in an extra blanket. I felt tears stream down my face.

PART TWO:
THIS THERAPIST LIKES TO PLAY

THE OFFICE

I had always enjoyed working as a psychotherapist. I enjoyed the daily travel to the office, the familiar faces, the ascent to the office which was situated on the second floor of a convent from the 1600s.

All the rooms for myself and my colleagues were round, a relic from the building's religious existence. Nuns had lived there for years, quietly walking along the hushed corridors, gliding smoothly up and down the stairs. It was now filled with a variety of different workspaces, creating a friendly environment, a community of people who loved working there.

Although not a large space in itself, my own office had two large sash windows, one of which opened up onto the college gardens. In the summer, the smell of cut grass and flowers wafted in each day from the large gardens. Every now and then a bee would come to investigate the room and I would escort him out of the window again. It was a peaceful place. A quiet place.

Then as things escalated in my everyday life outside of work, they escalated at work too. I would often go into my office and find things had been moved around. I found the window open when I knew I had closed it. I found my storage room had been opened, and papers and documents moved. I would find small dead animals left outside the office door. Papers, bits of wood, bits of grass, like offerings, left at the foot of the door of the office, to remind me, *we know where you work.*

Every day there seemed to be an additional intrusion.

My post, left on the desk in my office, would be opened.

Books would be left out and on the floor, items were constantly being moved around in the office.

Now that these new intrusions had begun, and since lockdown had enforced working from home for most people, my previously safe community building felt too empty. At night, walking back to my car along the top narrow road in the town where I worked, I would find my car open.

This continued for months at a time and continued even when working from office became normal again. Eventually I requested a change of locking systems on the door. A second lock was installed. The same thing happened. The continual, daily intrusions into my life. Now I would find my car tampered with, petrol taken, the wheel sometimes let down.

This was now part of life, at work, driving to work, driving home, at home, a regular interference, a sinister feeling of constantly being watched. It happened again and again and again, each time growing more and more sinister in nature. The cat-and-mouse game that had started was utterly exhausting in its incessant escalation, the ferocious intensity with which I was being targeted.

I started to keep client notes on my computer, fearing that they would be targeted by whoever was breaking into my office. The notes that I did write I wrote in shorthand, in a way only I would understand. Abbreviations, no names, obscure ways of writing, writing less and less over time, all became a way to ensure my client notes were not observable by anyone. Eventually I took down only the briefest amount of information necessary, storing it away in convoluted fashion. The impact on my professional practice was enormous. It was hard to believe that this had been orchestrated by someone of the same profession as myself. A profession that demanded, rightly, complete confidentiality. A profession that demanded, rightly, continued professional development and high standards.

A profession that is still, despite these high standards, unregulated and unaware of its own blind spot: its ego.

As time moved on, I started to fear the drive to the office. I felt huge trepidation walking up the stairs to my once-peaceful office, looking out onto the college gardens. The workspace that I had enjoyed and thrived in had been stolen, and I knew that if the intrusions did not stop, it was only a matter of time before I would have to leave.

I needed to see how Liam would respond to me now, after months and months of silence. I wanted to test out a theory.

THIS THERAPIST LIKES TO PLAY

Even though I knew it was true, I was looking for some confirmation, some acknowledgement that Liam was behind the chaos that had erupted around me. Even though I was able to follow the patterns around me and join the dots, I needed a sign that he was behind it all. I knew he would want it to be known in some way, that he could organize something this huge, this violent and illegal, and not be held accountable in any way. I knew it would appeal greatly to his diminished sense of self; it would be something he would be immensely proud of.

I decided to send him a message.

'Hello,' it started out. 'I just wanted to find out if you know any good play therapists in your area. A client of mine is looking for one and she lives in your neighbourhood.'

I waited for a response, a knot of fear growing steadily bigger by the minute.

The response came: 'I don't know of any play therapists, Suzanne, but this therapist likes to play…'

The response brought a sharp fizz of fear to my stomach.

It was all the confirmation I needed.

Liam's message was midway between an acknowledgement and a threat. Even in his message, he was playing with me, toying with me. The way he always had, the way he continued to play. Everything for him was a game. It was only a few words, but it was enough to confirm what I had always known.

From behind his farm gates, in the house with the hole in the floorboards, Liam was still stalking me.

He had started something designed to annihilate me. I knew he was a very convincing liar and skilled in the art of manipulation and deception. People were just objects to him, useful until proven otherwise.

I could sense where he would be employing his skills next. He was coming after my career. He was coming after my private practice. He was coming after my standing in the counselling community, the new life I had made for myself, and all the things in it that were so rewarding and fulfilling. He wanted to break all of it.

PSYCHE OF STALKING

In my ongoing attempt to exert some control over my situation, I searched randomly on Google for clues on understanding stalking behaviour. I came across a talk given by Dr. J. Reid Melody entitled 'Predatory Violence, Pattern of Behaviour and Proximal Warning Behaviours'. Melody talked about pathways to violence and a gestalt way of understanding what he terms 'Pattern Analysis'. The psychotherapist in me perked up. *Interesting,* I thought.

He listed patterns:

1: The grievance: what or who this person feels he has been wronged by

2: Ideation

3: Research and planning

4: Pre-attack

5: Probing and breaches including surveillance

6: Final behaviour

He says there is a continuing escalation and de-escalation along this continuum.

The object (victim) becomes the source of an unshakeable obsession. There is a pathological preoccupation with the victim and a deterioration of social and occupational functioning ensues. He mentioned surveillance. I felt I was constantly under surveillance, at every point of my day and night.

There is what he terms an extreme 'Overvalue Belief', coupled with delusion. The belief is amplified, and thinking becomes simplistic and binary and made absolute. The woman that said no becomes the bad object; the woman who said no becomes all women who say no. And all women who say no deserve this treatment.

Binary, absolute, simplistic.

This was my favourite take away from the lesson: any behaviour indicating a psychological desire to be pseudocommando or identifying oneself as an agent to advance a particular cause or behaviour system is predictive of attacks. Identification becomes a dark self-identity. This information, although terrifying, soothed me. It made me feel comforted: I was not the only one falling apart. Liam's pathological preoccupation was deteriorating. Good. I was able to put a shape not only on what drove Liam, but also what was driving those who participated in his game.

They were merely following a command, or joining up to receive validation, money, who knows. Liam, the one with the dark self-identity, was the one my mind struggled to understand.

Knowing this, I knew who I was dealing with, what the shape of their disturbances looked like, how dark they had allowed themselves to become. It all made sense.

The dark tetrad: Liam's personality ticked all the boxes.

Like all information I had found along the way, I felt uplifted by this talk, this unexpected gift of discovery. It felt both validating and empowering to have information. Real, usable information, like finding the mechanism with which to unlock something. Information like this was power. This man, talking about escalation and de-escalation of violence, describing the psyche of who and what I was dealing with in such clear, irrefutable terms, was a way through, a way forward.

THE HORSE

Now that I knew what I was up against, I knew I had to move out of my little estate that had become overgrown with individuals operating as a collective, becoming more and more violent, steered by Liam, who sat concealed behind the tall, stone walls of his farmhouse.

Moving into a new rental property in the depths of Covid was not an easy thing to do.

On the day that I decided to move, to escape the frenzy of activity surrounding me on the once- peaceful estate where I lived, there were six houses listed to rent in the area to which I had chosen to move.

One of the houses was located in a rural area, just outside of the busy town of Midleton. *Perfect,* I thought. *I'll be tucked away out of sight and hopefully they'll leave me alone.*

A few weeks later I had moved into the new house, enclosed by fields, a golf course, hedgerows and tall trees. I felt hidden from the world, and from the violence that had been following me. For a blissful month, I was left alone.

The world started to feel less grey and more open. I walked along the country roads and breathed in the strange feeling of being left alone and unobserved.

In the field next to the house was a horse. As well as dark and beautiful, she was friendly, gentle, calm, galloping towards the opposite fence every evening when her owner would do the feeding round. Watching her in this tranquil place felt soothing, restful and gave me a sense that life had returned to normal. I sat each morning in the hot summer, drinking coffee, watching her graze on the long grasses, swishing her tail backwards and forwards. I felt myself coming back from a frozen state of terror to an almost relaxed way of being.

One day, coming home from a walk, I noticed a car approaching me on a country road. I moved to the side of the road, and it slowed down. The car moved to the middle of the road and stopped. I felt some murmur of disquiet emerge from within me. It started moving forward slowly, slowly, inching its way towards me. Now, almost directly in front of me, the windows started closing. I looked into the car as it stopped next to me, engine running. The windows were blacked out, making it impossible to see inside. I walked past, my heart banging. The sweat ran down my face. I wanted to run, but I stopped myself. I wanted to see what would happen if I carried on walking slowly.

The car remained in the middle of the road. After a while, it slowly eased forward, and gradually disappeared round the corner. I was nearing the turnoff to the little track leading homeward, and sped up my pace. Just as I reached the narrow lane, the same car stopped alongside me, engine running, windows up.

I knew it was the start of something. It was a warning sign.

After that, life became a daily nightmare. Coming home from work, I would see the shower floor was wet, my towel, also wet, placed in the middle of the floor.

The once-peaceful hum of the boiler now became a loud, intrusive noise that went on and off, and on and off. In the end it grew so loud it would wake up my daughter.

'What on earth is happening now?' she would ask, frustrated at the eternal intrusion into our lives.

The tap started to drip, on and off and on and off; the gas heater was on when I returned from being out somewhere, when I knew I had shut it off. The electricity bills started to spiral, more and more units being used despite the fact that I was never in the house.

The car was being tampered with. I was followed everywhere again: down country roads, meeting friends, going to yoga … followed, harassed, stalked, targeted again and again and again.

The gentle, calm horse became hostile. When I approached her, she would rear up wildly, pawing at the air, snorting with rage. Instead of taking an apple offered to her, she would charge at the wooden fence, teeth bared, ears flattened back against her massive head.

I wondered if she had been drugged. She seemed at times like a horse on cocaine. Her tail would be lifted into a high arc, her neck up and back, charging wildly, recklessly around the field. This was not normal behaviour for her, or for any horse I'd previously encountered.

I know horses. I'd had a wild pony once, as a teenager. She had been afraid of nothing, inclined to jump high fences and take off at a tangent on the forest track we would explore, and she would throw me off her back at any given time. But even she in all her wildness did not come close to the horse in the field.

I suspected she had been targeted because we had a bond, and anything I was close to or valued was a potential target.

I considered going to the authorities.

The conversation in my head went something like this:

'I think the horse has been drugged,' I would say.

'Oh right, ok,' they'd respond. 'How do you know she has been drugged?'

I would say something like, 'I don't know. I am saying I *think* she has been drugged.'

And then I would imagine their familiar response might be, 'Ah but we can't do anything without any evidence.'

*

THE HORSE

The house nightmare continued unabated. There were nights when I tried to sleep, my door locked, windows tightly fastened shut. A knock, knock on the bathroom window would wake me up. Falling asleep again, it would once more wake me up. On and on. I would wake and move rooms, this time certain I would be left alone. A knock, knock on the roof woke me this time. I would settle to sleep and again it would wake me, on and on. I would go outside to see who was there, but only the stars and the black night were visible.

The once-promising rural setting was now proving to be an opportunity to torment me further. At night, I would some-times hear footsteps on the roof. Not one pair of footsteps, but two. I imagined two participants, high on cocaine, laughing at the sheer insanity of the job posted on the dark web: *People without a fear of heights needed for intimidation and harassment. May require some rough sleeping and a horse to contend with.*

They were having the time of their lives. They were enjoying this game of cat and mouse, this secret experiment.

I was not. The strategies worsened over the summer. I would leave the front door open, only to find an array of bugs and spiders thrown into the house, invading every corner of my living space. I started to leave the door shut at all times, always waiting for the next level of invasion, the newest strategy to be concocted. I started to see scratches on my body, a scratch on my face every now and then. I wondered how it had arrived there.

During that summer, I awoke to find my eye socket swollen. Each morning I struggled to see out of my eye, trying to douse the swelling with cold water and aloe vera. Eventually it settled. I then woke to find my face covered with small red dots. The effect was rather like chickenpox, but it wasn't chickenpox. It was as if someone had come into the room while I was asleep, and poked at my face, making it swollen, red, bumpy.

I decided to start recording these facial wounds and took images of them.

Years later, in an attempt to get the police to understand the level of violence I was experiencing, I sent these images to the head of police. I imagined him opening the envelope and seeing my face, riddled with bumps, my eye socket swollen, and wondering what I was doing sending it to him.

Some acts of violence are hard to explain. A bruise in an abusive relationship looks like abuse. It looks like someone was hit, thrown against a wall. But the acts of violence happening to me were concealed. They were made to look like anything could have caused them. If I couldn't get the police to understand I was being stalked, there was no way I could explain how my face became so disfigured. A photograph, however, could convey a small degree of the level of invasion happening to me. I was being violently targeted, and I wanted someone to see it.

During the day, having applied liberal amounts of concealer on the bumps, I would see my clients, and attempt to leave my ongoing nightmare at home. Some days it was possible. Often it was not. The truth was that my private practice was being severely impacted by the goings-on at the house, the nightly intrusions, the daily sequences of bizarre and frightening break-ins. My concentration was beginning to falter, and I started to forget things as the escalation of violence seeped into my daily work. I was followed to work, I was followed from work. My life seemed to be contracting.

Friends tried to reassure me while family members were mostly kept out of the loop of what was going on. I felt I was drowning, secretly, silently, and nobody could see me being pulled further and further from shore.

The worst, however, was yet to come.

CARS

The fascination with my car began at roughly the same time as the stalking itself. I would frequently find the car had been tampered with, the tyres punctured, the windshield wipers split in two. I would never really know what new damage would await me as I walked to my car each morning. The two PIR cameras that I had installed outside the house were pointless. It took me about two weeks to realize that my phone had been hacked and the devices switched off.

The car was old, and an easy enough target. It had a prehistoric locking mechanism and no alarm. I would always find it open, oozing the smell of slurry.

This way of tampering with my car remained a pattern for a while. I would emerge from a day out in the city or from the shops and sure enough, the car would have been tampered with in some way or another.

Once I moved to the second house, the pattern escalated into something more serious.

Now, driving to work, my engine light would light up, at random intervals. I would switch the car off for a few minutes and the light would go off. Driving again, it would switch on, off, on, off. The on-switch would make the car judder and splutter, jolting, almost stopping. On and on and on, all the way to work and all the way back. All the way to the shops and all the way back.

I took the car to the mechanic.

'Nothing wrong here,' he said, giving my car the all-clear from an engine test.

'Great,' I would say, knowing full well it would just be tampered with again.

And it was, again and again and again, making my trips to work or to visit friends stressful and anxiety-inducing experiences. My daughter noticed it too. She would watch as the car juddered and jolted its way to and from the places we would go. She would remark on the way in which it was being tampered with, continually. We would attempt to laugh about it, but it was a hollow laugh. It wasn't funny.

Deciding later that year to upgrade my car to a newer model, one that was fully covered by a car dealership, I felt safer, more able to relax when driving to work.

Only a new pattern developed: diesel theft. Filling up the car, I would park it at a local shop and arrive back at the car half an hour later. Sure enough, the diesel marker had dropped, and again at the next stop. I imagined Liam and his associates selling the collected diesel on some black-market system. Or placing it into their own cars, pleased at the thought that not only were they stealing my sleep, my waking hours, my work, my colleagues, my friends, my identity, my source of joy, my life, now they were also stealing my fuel.

'Ha ha,' the gutless thieves would gleefully chuckle.

I imagined the subtle nods, side eyes, the undercurrent of secrecy in silent exchanges, communication from their participants, their slaves and underdogs, nonentities of the dark world that bolstered up their own nonexistent feelings of importance, built on a shadow.

They are all still, and always have been, painfully aware of their own lack of importance, their own impotence.

The real secret of the network is that they know, deep down, that they are nothing, amongst nobodies.

THE PARTICIPANTS

The network of nobodies included participants from all walks of life.

The ringleaders had bought most of them with a lie and a bribe. They'd told few of the participants the full story. They'd given levels of information, and told most participants something about me that was untrue or given them highly compromising (and presumably entertaining) images of me. Some participants had been coerced, but most were paid and perfectly willing accomplices.

At the heart of the strategy used was the relentless drive to make me seem like the problem. Anything they could accuse me of, anything that could be fabricated, to make me seem like the offender, was attempted. It was and is still the primary way in which this game works.

Most of the participants and co-offenders had been kept in the dark by the brothers about the extent of what had happened, and none had been told the real reason behind the drive to stalk me and surround me like a pack of wolves.

They kept the real grievance secret.

They had buried the truth long ago and put in its place a convenient story.

Because the accomplices had been given a 'reason', I became an object. I was not a person; I was a non-human, someone available for experimentation because 'she deserves it'.

It's a strange kind of reasoning, but it was effective nonetheless.

The action of stalking and tracking me simply added to the dehumanizing effect. I was just an object and all of those around me to whom I was close were similar targets also.

The participants lost sight of me as a person.

From a psychological perspective, this was fascinating. From a *target's* perspective, though, it was terrifying.

All of the players in this game were, and still are, delusional.

The delusion of grandeur, or overvalue belief, of their own significance, still unites them now in a common goal.

Because now I am writing my story. Because this secret entertainment is being exposed, they've had to change the way they work: they are hacking my computer, they use their phones with discretion and seldom in plain sight. I imagine a different code is being used.

In my mind's eye, a red flag waving, hoisted over bridges, gently billowing in the summer air.

Cork colours.

THE WOMAN ON THE RADIO

Driving home from a busy day at the office, I found myself listening to the radio. A woman was telling the presenter how different people were following her up and down Patrick Street, taking photographs of her. She described how she would leave her apartment and walk down the main street, only to notice that people who were not known to her would surreptitiously be taking her photograph. Initially, she went on to say, she was confused and alarmed. Was she imagining this? Was this really being aimed at her? Over time, this became more and more obvious as the volume of people following her increased.

This happened at any time of day and continued for months. She was constantly being watched and followed. At the time of the interview, it was still continuing. She described her journey in dealing with this kind of unwanted attention as a nightmare.

Navigating the narrow road that led to my house, I was transported. Here was another person going through a similar ordeal of being followed relentlessly.

It began, she said, when she started a blog which detailed her weight-loss transformation. Eventually, she found out that images of her were being posted online, alongside negative and damaging commentary.

She stayed calm on the radio and the radio hosts commended her for her ability to remain level-headed, regardless of the fact that she was being pursued by a large number of people taking images of her every day, all day.

But what alternative does she have? I wondered.

I wanted to talk to this woman, to ask her how she managed the effects of being followed, pursued, kept under close scrutiny, every day.

This snapshot of her life is still with me now, in 2023.

Even now I can hear her speak clearly, her voice not devoid of emotion, but rather emotion fiercely controlled. She has learned how to contain her rage, her pain, her fear of what this will do to her over time.

In a strange way, I felt better having heard her speak about her struggles. I felt less alone with mine. I felt validated. *This kind of thing has happened to other people,* I thought, the full weight of that realization still sinking in.

We do not speak of these things. They cut through the space of silence surrounding the secret network, and something strange happens when we break silence on their tacit codes, the arrangements we have not agreed to, the games into which we have not entered willingly.

I drove slowly up the narrow boreen leading to the cottage, tall grasses spilling over the edges and onto the road. The horse was in the field, alert, ears pricked forward. I stopped by the post box at the top of the driveway, knowing that most of my post would have disappeared or been opened. The post box, which had been smashed and replaced numerous times, was empty.

I arrived home in a daze. It took a while for the information to sink in, that somewhere in Cork, there was someone who knew what it was like to be intruded upon, viciously by a large group of ever-changing people, all united in one cause: stalking her. Perhaps not in the same way. She had not spoken of house break-ins or car tampering, or people slowly annihilating her ability to work in a place she had grown to really love, but the mental battleground that she portrayed, that is what we had in common.

She knew what it felt like to go to war every day, with an invisible web gradually encircling her.

PROXY STALKING

After listening to the woman on the radio, and after months of bewildering and terrifying behaviour which had something in common with what she was describing, I decided to do some research into what this kind of violence was known as.

In Ireland, it all is termed 'harassment'. I wanted to know what it was known as globally.

Initially I came across 'cyberstalking'. I scrolled down the list of all the identifiable behaviours associated with it and found that I could tick most of the boxes. Most of the behaviour listed had been thrown my way, or was currently ongoing. I had no idea at that point that everything was going to become a lot worse, but it somewhat described what I was experiencing.

I still had no understanding of the broader mechanism at play. The people being used on the ground. The delivery drivers, the post that was going astray, all of the many, many people in this game. I needed a better understanding of it. This felt too much like organized crime to neatly fit the cyberstalking definition. It did underline that stalking behaviours included surveillance, life invasion, intimidation, and interference. It is an obsessive, fixated, and unwanted series of intrusive actions that, taken individually, do not necessarily constitute a crime, but collectively, do. But I had had my house broken into, repeatedly. I had been harmed physically. There were hundreds, if not thousands, of people that had been used and continued to be used as part of this experiment. This was not *only* cyberstalking.

Then a friend sent me a link to an article on proxy stalking, or multiple-perpetrator stalking. There seemed to be a large body of research that had been done on this behaviour. The information I read somehow came a bit closer to describing what it felt like, what the mechanisms were in this game.

Logan and Walker write: 'Instances of multiple perpetrator stalking have been identified … as proxy stalking, cases where a stalker can enlist willing friends or associates to aid in their behaviour, they can coerce, bribe or intimidate unwilling associates or even trick the victim's friends or family into gaining access to the victim … proxy stalkers took the place of the primary stalker … aiding in the stalking activities … Victimization by proxy stalkers could represent heightened consequences for victims, as having multiple people watching you, following or harassing them could intensify their feelings of fear and worry, and indicates their primary stalker is committed to continuing the relationship.' (Logan & Walker, 2017).

The last sentence stayed with me for a long time afterwards: 'And indicates their primary stalker is committed to continuing the relationship.'

Committed. The sentence sent a spidery chill up my arms. That was exactly how it felt. That all the associates had either been bribed or coerced and really were an extension to the primary stalker and his need for control and an unbreakable, obsessive will to have a relationship with me. The last sentence that I read encapsulated my entire history with Liam. The caged, trapped feeling that I experienced in his company, the determination to get me back and control me that I have felt ever since.

My research opened a door. I finally had been given a way of seeing, or understanding, what was happening to me. I thought of the many van drivers, delivery drivers, truck drivers that had ceaselessly circled me while I was out walking, or in my house, or in my estate. For years I had felt that somehow these were not coincidental drivers, these were co-offenders, accomplices, associates. They were an extension of the person behind all of this: Liam.

Even more chilling was research I discovered that demonstrated that 'crimes committed by groups of associates, or co-offenders, are more likely than those perpetrated by single offenders to involve weapons or result in an injury' (Lantz, 2018)[2].

I thought of the long list of violent behaviour that had been inflicted on me. It felt like a daily assault, a pattern of abuse that was determined to physically and psychologically hurt me. At this point, the brothers and their associates were only warming up. There was so much more that would come my way, and would hurt both me and my family. I would think back often to that research and again and again acknowledge its validity.

One of the researchers I had come across had written, 'Police intervention by talking to or warning the perpetrator(s) is effective at disrupting the stalking situation, highlighting the need for police officers to understand multiple perpetrator stalking and be able to adequately help these victims.'[3] (NGO, 2020) .

I found myself becoming intensely angry as I read more and more about the importance of acknowledging stalking as stalking, and the importance of police intervention. My life was being invaded; there was massive surveillance of me, of my family, occurring; we were being harassed incessantly; and everything I owned, everything I had worked hard for, was being interfered with relentlessly. There were lies being spread about me that were harmful and injurious.

---

2 Lantz, B., 'The consequences of crime in company: Co-offending, victim–of-fender relationship, and quality of violence.' *Journal of Interpersonal Violence, 36*(7-8).

3 Ngo, F. T. (2020). Stalking victimization: Examining the impact of police action and inaction on victim-reported outcome. *Journal of Police and Criminal Psychology, 35*(2), 146156

THIS THERAPIST LIKES TO PLAY

Had anyone ever darkened the door of the perpetrators?

No.

Had they ever been questioned, warned, followed, intruded upon?

No.

Were they likely to be warned, ever? Investigated?

No.

Why?

Because in Ireland there is no law against stalking.

And because of that there is no understanding of stalking and because of that, there is no understanding of multiple-perpetrator stalking.

With the fog of uncertainty lifted, and an ability to name what was happening to me in its place, I became angry at being forced into a position of helplessness. The lack of legislation to help me – and presumably thousands of women in a similar situation in Ireland – was dangerous.

WEBSITE PORN

It was not the first time I had been to the police station, and it would not be the last. This time, I thought, this time I really had something. A website listing all the therapists working with me had been hacked and large amounts of porn placed on it. At the same time, my name, linked with the name of another musician, had been scattered all over the internet, telling the world that I was 'available for sex hook-ups at a website near you'. This was a crime. I had screenshots, I had proof, I had evidence, and I had it all available, ready to be investigated. *At last,* I thought, *here's something that is going to change everything.*

I could not have been more mistaken.

The detective looked at me with a jaded eye as I followed him into the station inquiry room.

'Yes?' he said.

I started telling him the same thing I had told many people in his position: that I was being followed and stalked and harassed by a group of people and they were in the process of radically undermining me, spreading damaging rumours about me and ruining my career.

I showed him the porn shots from our website. I showed him the screenshots littering the internet with my name on it. He seemed concerned.

He told me in a reassuring tone that he would have a look at the website and screenshots and get back to me once he had done a bit of digging. Walking out of the station, I felt a sense of huge relief. Here, finally, was something being done. I had managed to find someone who understood what was happening. It was all going to be ok.

After a few days, having heard nothing from this particular detective, I returned to the station. I asked the person at the desk if I could have a word and a few minutes later he returned, the detective following closely.

He ushered me into the interview room. He seemed less interested than the time before. I felt that I had to speak quickly to hold his interest. I asked him if he had followed up on any of the leads.

'Look,' he said, sounding tired, 'I don't want to besmirch your character, but I don't believe you.'

Stunned, I sat and stared at him. I wanted to cry. I wanted to shout. I did neither.

'But did you look into it at all?' I asked.

He seemed reluctant to say whether he had done or not. 'I don't think there is anything there to be concerned about,' he said.

'But my name is all over the internet inviting people, the world, to click onto a sex hook-up site so that they can have sex with me,' I responded, starting to feel that same desperation taking hold. I felt I was falling.

'There is nothing we can do about that and it probably has nothing to do with … this', he said, lamely waving his hand at my case file.

I knew the conversation was over. I knew the interest in following up this lead had fallen by the wayside; it was sinking quickly and I along with it.

Outside, the summer sky was a clear blue. I felt dizzy and numb.

Why did he not investigate something so tangible, so obvious?

I felt a cold weight press down on me, trampling me into the pavement. The familiar sweaty nausea rose and settled in as I walked slowly to the car. Even when I had evidence, it was viewed with such disdain. Like an inconvenience that needed to be squashed.

*

Each visit went like this:

'Well,' he says, 'tell me, briefly, what it is that is happening.'

'My ex used to stalk me for years. That has stopped but now instead of one person following me, a number of people are following me around, with their phones, tracking my every move, and I am afraid. It's called proxy stalking.'

'Riiiiiight,' I hear the person think. *She really has lost the plot. People are following her.* 'Which people? Why are they following you?'

'I have really no idea apart from the fact that my ex has a grievance and wants to get even,' I venture.

'Why would they all follow you?'

'Because they are getting paid and having fun. Why else would someone do anything like this? It's like trolling except more sadistic and sinister.'

'Riiiight. Well, what you need to do is …'

'Have you done …?'

'Why don't you …?'

The correct term for this of course is victim-blaming, making me the problem, but I did not feel like having one of those conversations. I just needed this person to understand that bad people do bad things, and it just so happens that I was the current target.

The conversation went flat, every time.

I knew the words I wanted to put on this experience – this experiment, this game, this secret – but they never did it justice.

A MAP OF THE MIND

Before I moved out of the small estate, before I lived in the cottage surrounded by fields. I decided, against my better judgement, to pay Liam a visit. It was the 28th June 2020. In my mind this was a ridiculous, stupid, terrifying thing that needed to be stopped. Perhaps it was out of sheer desperation that I drove there that morning. Looking back, I would not do the same thing now.

Driving up the narrow road to his farm, I felt on edge. I stopped before his driveway, and turned in, expecting to see his fat face appear from the little outhouse he used as a counselling office. 'The best counselling space in Cork,' he used to say, over and over and over again.

Nothing moved on the farm. His car was not there. I decided to drive up the backroads of his farm to fields above the farm-house. He had taken me there before, placing me in front of a large herd of cows.

'Just wave,' he'd said. 'They don't bite.'

If he is stalking me, which he is, he will know that I have been to his house, and I know that he will magically appear.

He did appear.

Driving past, he seemed not to notice me. I jammed on the brakes and turned to face the direction he was driving. *If he is following me, then he will do the same,* I thought.

And he did.

A few minutes later his car approached from the opposite direction he was driving in, and slowed down.

'Suzanne,' he said, the icy coldness in his voice still present. 'How nice to see you,' he lied. 'I was just going to the house. What a coincidence to see you here,' he lied again.

Out of the corner of my eye, an old silver 4x4 belonging to a man who lived in the same estate that I lived in came into view. I had been keeping track of the registration numbers of the cars in the estate. I recognised his car immediately.

That's odd, I thought. *Why on earth is he here?* I caught sight of the man with his short grey hair and weasel-like expression. He seemed to not want to be recognised, and sped down a different road that led from the one we were on.

Liam and I were both stopped on the narrow country road, our cars facing each other. The windows of the cars were down, and there was only an arm's length between the opened front window of his car and mine.

My heart was racing, the palms of my hands clammy with sweat.

'You have to stop this,' I said, staring directly into his eyes. They were cold, dead, empty.

'I don't know what you mean.' He smirked. His cold, dead eyes bore straight through me. They filled me with terror.

'You know exactly what I mean,' I said.

He laughed. A cold, mocking laugh.

We sat, cars idling, caught in a deadlock in the middle of the road. I stared at him, and he stared back. Smirking. Laughing. Grinning. His cold, expressionless eyes unblinking.

The sweat was pouring down my back. In the sweltering heat of the day, I felt the temperature rise in the car. My heart was beating loudly, my mind was racing. I could see he was enjoying watching me struggle, powerless to change what was happening to me.

Eventually, I looked away, and drove off. I felt numb.

It was real. *All of this is really real. He is doing it all, and enjoying every second, without remorse. It's a game he is playing. Cat and*

*mouse. He is toying with me. Watching me suffer, struggle, beg and
plead with him to stop this. He is building a secret network: the
neighbour, the man in the car four doors down, people who live near
to me, and those that don't. Gathering more and more participants
and unifying them in a common goal.*

I thought of him watching me try to fall asleep, frozen with
terror; laughing at the thought of someone breaking into my house
and watching me sleep. My life had become a nightmare and he
had found his greatest purpose in stalking me: slowly watching
me give up on life. I thought of his eyes staring at me. Devoid of
anything, sadistic, obsessively driven to keep hurting me, keep
following me, keeping a safe distance so as not to get caught.

As I drove home, I could not shake the image of the man in
the car – the same man who lived four houses away from me in
my small estate – hurriedly driving away, like somebody caught
at the scene of a crime. It was no coincidence that they had both
been driving down the same narrow country road on the same
day, at the same time.

That moment illuminated something in short, sharp succession:
they were working together.

I had learned some time before that this person was involved
in some tech-related industry, and presumably had the skills that
Liam needed to hack my computer and track me down each day,
all day. I imagined he was paid accordingly for his services. The
narrow road led to another piece of farmland, a green shed where
they could plan in secrecy the next attack on me.

They could advance the steady, secret accumulation of
participants.

The next day, I decided to talk to a colleague, and let her
know what had transpired the previous day. I knew deep down
he would try his utmost to turn this visit against me.

As we stood talking that morning, her phone began to ring. I
could see that it was Liam. He rang again. And again.

'Let's see what he says,' I said.

A while later, she re-emerged from her office. 'Apparently he is concerned about you. Apparently he thinks you are unwell, unhinged, coming up with strange theories about him.

When I didn't agree with him, when I contradicted him, he threatened me. He said he would have to bring this to the attention of the organization and to the police.'

This confirmed everything. This five-minute conversation exposed him, in every way possible. It exposed his darkness. Wanting to turn people against me, he lied. Every conceivable sort of lie imaginable. If the lie was not taken in and absorbed, if the person did not agree that I was the problem, he would turn quickly and bare his teeth. He would threaten. 'Bring this to the attention of the organization and the police ...' I could see now why I wasn't having any luck in that department. And by 'organization', Liam meant the counselling organization to which we all belonged.

I felt profoundly relieved at my colleague's remark. I felt her standing by me, where so many others had not. I felt less alone, bolstered by her solidarity in the face of being threatened. I could see that she was taken aback by his threat, but she did not allow it to get in the way. I could feel her support and her resolve, and I felt protected.

That conversation provided us with a map that had been laid out for us both to see. A map of a dark mind, insistent on being obeyed. A convincing liar, an insistent liar approaching in a pseudo-friendly way. Anyone standing in his way would be threatened. 'If you don't go along with my version of events, I will come after you in every way possible.'

Lie, threaten, threaten, lie. His remark also revealed that he felt secure enough of his position within the organization that his threat would hold some degree of weight were he to proceed with it. What it also suggested strongly was that were he to visit the police, *his* voice would be heard.

THIS THERAPIST LIKES TO PLAY

This was what I was up against.
This is what I am up against still.

COUNSELLING BODIES

Growing increasingly tired of the endless stalking, again and again I communicated with the governing body of the association that I belonged to, to see if they could help.

In my letter, I asked that due to my computer being hacked, they not link in my letter.

A few weeks later, I received an email, with the original correspondence duly linked, telling me that unfortunately there was nothing they could do. *We do not have a bullying and harassment policy and there is really no further action that can be taken.*

A few months on, I wrote to the head of the organization, telling her explicitly what had been started by two registered counsellors who were part of the organization.

I never heard back from her, but received a letter from the organization to say that the matter had been passed to a different committee. A few weeks later, I received a letter to say that the committee had decided to not proceed with any action.

I felt that same deflated feeling with which I have now become so familiar. They didn't want to know. Nobody, it seemed, wanted to know about this dark, thorny nest of thieves and liars, psychopaths, sadists, narcissists, people of the shadows. *I am on my own,* I was told, again and again and again.

Eventually, I thought, *eventually they will destroy my reputation and gradually pull any remaining clients away from me. Eventually I will leave this room, with its windows opening up onto the college gardens, because it will all be too much.*

THIS THERAPIST LIKES TO PLAY

Eventually happens sooner than I imagine.

THE VISITOR

Late one night, I heard the sound of footsteps coming from downstairs, just a gentle shush shush of feet padding the surface of the kitchen. I threw on a jumper and silently descended the stairs. Coming round the corner, I saw someone leave the kitchen via the back door.

Usually, I kept it bolted and the windows securely locked. By securely locked, what I mean is locked with a number of additional safety features. Locking the house and ensuring it was not broken into had been an ongoing saga since this nightmare had begun. Locks, I had discovered, were not very useful. Changing locks had proved even more futile.

But I knew the back door had been bolted, which was difficult to unbolt – or so I thought in my various stages of denial.

The door closed. A man, about the height and build of my previous neighbour, had exited the house, disappearing into the black of the night. There were no lights outside the house and it was easy to slip into the surrounding fields, away from the property. The lounge smelled of hay and manure. A dank, rancid smell hung in the air, bits of dirt had fallen on the floor. It smelled like someone who had been sleeping rough.

I called the police. An hour later, they arrived. I began to explain how I had seen someone leave the house. Nothing had been taken. I explained that I was afraid. I explained how I was being stalked and targeted and had moved house to escape. I explained and explained and explained.

Politely taking notes, the two policemen left a while later, promising the return of a detective the next morning.

The detective arrived, statement book in hand. I walked him through the proceedings of the night before, saying that I had seen someone leave the house. Someone had been sleeping on my couch while I slept in the room above. It was part of an organized strategy to stalk and terrorize me.

It was pretty straightforward. Breaking and entering. I presumed it was a crime. I presumed there would be fingerprints taken or some sort of investigation.

I was wrong.

After writing for a while, the detective seemed to falter at the words, 'I saw someone leave the house.' 'Are you sure?' he said. 'You actually saw someone leave the house?'

'Yes,' I said, baffled that I had to repeat myself. I felt that familiar sinking feeling take hold.

'But how could you see someone leave the house?' he asked.

'I saw someone leave via the back door.'

The conversation went on for a while. Eventually he left. No fingerprints taken, no follow-up. I sat on the front porch, curled up as tightly as possible. Was nothing going to be done?

Why was there no follow up?

The question still remains with me today.

What was it that I had failed to express?

How could I have made myself understood?

Someone was in my house. Someone I did not want to be there. This was part of an ongoing intrusion into my life. Stalking and proxy stalking. A violent campaign which was obsessive, intrusive, dangerous and unwanted.

Why was that not a crime?

Why was there a persistent recurrence of people breaking into my house and nothing ever done about it?

Was this normal? Was this the way other people experienced their homes being broken into?

If nothing is taken from a house, is breaking and entering not a crime?

If just one person says someone had broken into their house, is that not believable?

Why was nothing I said ever taken seriously?

THE DETECTIVE

On December 31st 2020, growing weary of continually followed and targeted, I visited the local police station. On the advice of a retired police person, I took a full statement to hand over. It was eleven pages long, and contained a fraction of the ongoing, daily events that had beset me for the past year. It was an unusually long visit, and by the time I emerged, I could feel the muscles in my neck were stiff, and my feet were cold. It did not feel like New Year's Eve. It felt like a replay of something that had become stuck, the wheels refusing to turn. It felt like I was sliding back a year, not moving forward, resolutions in hand, steady and able to pursue goals and dreams. It felt like I was slowly drowning.

I was surprised, then, that on the back of the visit I was allocated a detective.

The detective, I discovered, was a woman. *Great,* I thought. *She will be able to help me.*

I was contacted in mid-January 2021 and a day and time was arranged to meet her.

It was a bitterly cold January morning when I arrived at the police station. Trees lining the narrow street leading to the station seemed weary and bereft. Their empty branches were mawed and stunted with the cold. Crows pecked determinedly at boxes of leftover fish and chips lying on the pavement. It was a dull day and the sky seemed closed over and impenetrable.

I had come to resent the familiarity of the building, just as

I had come to resent the way in which the same response was given to me again and again and again.

Finally, the detective showed me into the small interview room, the one where the table and chairs had been secured to the floor, presumably in order that nobody could, in a fit of rage, pick them up and smash them against the window. Later, months on, I would come to know that rage. That feeling of wanting to smash things, anything, everything, through the window, against the door, against the hard concrete floor, smashing things and breaking things as though the fragments of whatever was broken could, momentarily, provide relief. Relief from rage, relief from not being believed, relief from fear.

Rage and fear are an odd mix. They take the reins of the nervous system deep in the body and rattle with all their might. The combined effect is unnerving, the body looking for something to crash into and steady itself, finding only dust.

The detective looked at me accusingly. I was interrupting her day. I was an unwelcome addition to her workload. I was already a problem: someone to be dismissed as soon as possible.

I began to tell her how I was being stalked.

'We don't use that word,' she said, abruptly. 'We don't say "stalked". There is no such thing as stalking. We say "harassed".'

A rattle of a snake, hissing, the bell of alarm starts to ring, deep down. 'I'm being harassed as well as stalked,' I said. 'They are *not* the same thing.'

They are not the same thing. They are not the same thing. The words tumble in my mouth, rolling around and around until they come out, falling flat on the hard, silver table. The point of contention on which all other visits to the police station had centred, turning and spinning and blurring the lines between this kind of intrusion and something else. Something this big, this harmful, this terrifying had a name, and its name was stalking.

She appeared belligerent. Like someone who doesn't like to be disagreed with. Ignoring my comment, she said, 'The police deal in black and white. Do you have any evidence?'

I started to panic. That same feeling of falling, of disappearing, of becoming silent, was making its way deep into my throat.

'Yes,' I whispered. I was afraid now; she had decided to not believe me before I had even started to explain. 'I have had my house broken into,' I said. 'I have had my car broken into. I have been followed around wherever I walk and whatever I do.'

'But what evidence do you have?' she interrupted loudly. Abruptly. Aggressively.

'There were no fingerprints taken,' I said. 'There were no statements taken. Nothing was ever investigated.'

She seemed to disconnect at this point. Looking at her watch, she said, 'I need to go now, I'll be in touch.' She never referenced the eleven-page statement that I had handed in, or what I had written in it. She seemed to be ignorant of its contents and the gravity of my statement.

The wind outside cut my face with its shards of ice. I walked slowly, my hands and feet numb with cold. For a moment I forgot where the car was parked. Was it along the side street, I wondered. Feeling relieved once I had found it, I slid into the front seat, letting out a deep sigh. I had placed so much hope on this visit. This person, This experience. This was going to be the one that could help me. This was going to be the one that could make a difference.

A few weeks went by, and I heard nothing from the detective. No phone call, no follow-up. Deafening silence. I called the police station and was told she was not there.

A few weeks later I phoned again, and we had a short conversation. In it she said that these things take time, and that I was going to be wasting my time as well as hers by continuing to phone her.

That was February.

In March, I tried again. I phoned the police station to see what was happening regarding the investigation. Not receiving an answer, I visited the station and explained that I had been given a detective who never called me. The officer listened closely and turned to go, saying, 'I'll be back in a while.'

I waited. Soon after, he reappeared, followed by the detective. She looked dejected and annoyed that her day had been interrupted.

We sat in the interview room, and I asked what had been done to further the investigation into my case.

She said, 'These things take time, Suzanne. I am waiting to receive your GP notes.'

I took a deep breath. I had been in contact with my GP the day before. She had already sent my notes to the detective weeks prior to our meeting.

'You have my GP notes,' I said, trying hard to remain polite.

The detective said nothing. She stared at me and then at the table in the room.

I had caught her out, yet she remained unapologetic and even more determined to ignore my attempts at being helped, at being protected.

The police officer who sat opposite me appeared uncomfortable, awkward. He seemed to know that what was happening was not right. He knew she had been caught out. In an attempt to show solidarity with the detective, he said, 'She has been very busy on a case. She is trying to find the identity of a dead woman found on an abandoned train line in the town.'

The discovery had set the small town ablaze with speculation and horror. Everybody wanted to know the story, *her* story.

My head was spinning by the end of the meeting. I was parched and my throat was on fire. Driving home, I found myself replaying the conversation over and over again. Had she really lied to me? It was hard to believe. Was she trying to cover up for the fact that no work had been done on this? Why was it that every time I visited the police station, I was left with the message that I was the problem?

What had happened to my eleven-page statement? It seemed to have vanished from view.

I never heard from her again. In May that year, five months after having been assigned this detective, I visited the police station again, and again, and again. I was finally told that there had been a breakdown in communication between the detective and myself. And despite this admission, I never heard from her again. I also never heard what became of the extensive statement I had painstakingly written and handed in.

After that, the visits to the police station became less and less frequent. I often wondered to myself what kind of person I had to be, in order to be heard and believed and taken seriously. It was of course very inconvenient that clues as to the identity of the people responsible for this were not left on a daily basis outside my home, or inside my home, but even when they were, I stopped calling the police station. Even when the facts were flying high like an enormous red flag in the Cork city air, even then, I could not bring myself to call the police station.

In the end, the total number was forty-two.

Forty-two times I visited the police to explain that I was being stalked, harassed, that I had no privacy, that I was being viciously targeted, constantly surveilled and I was deeply afraid.

Forty-two times I was refused any help.

And then I stopped calling the police.

THE SUPERMARKET

Because I was so afraid, because I needed protection, because the police were not protecting me, I decided to write to the owner of a large supermarket in the nearby town. I wanted to see if he could recommend any private security guards or companies who I could contact and employ.

I often noticed the security people that worked in the supermarket. They were tall, lean, and had eyes like hawks. They missed nothing. They were always courteous, and remained pleasant but professional. I needed someone like that keeping an eye on the house where I was living. My cottage in the middle of the countryside, surrounded by trees, shrubs and large, grassy fields.

I wrote him a letter. It went something like this:

Dear Sir/Shop owner. I am currently being stalked and need to hire protective services such as a security guard as I am afraid. If you know of any such security people and / or companies that you would recommend, please could you let me know.
Kind Regards
Suzanne Joubert
[telephone number]

I walked into the shop one afternoon, en-route to my private practice in another town, and handed the letter to someone who worked there.

'Please give this to your boss. It's quite urgent,' I said. I went to work and set about my day seeing clients, relieved that I had taken a further step to try and protect myself. I switched off my phone, which I always did, and began working.

At around 7.00 p.m., I switched my phone back on, and was surprised to see six missed calls. They were all from the same number. Instead of listening to the messages, I immediately called the number. It was the police station.

'Yes,' said the police officer. 'We received an urgent call from the owner of the local supermarket. He was worried about you. He was concerned for your safety. He wanted us to help you. He said you were being stalked.'

Trying not to shout at the person on the phone, I said, 'Yes, I am being stalked. I have been trying to say so for a while now. Nobody is hearing me, nobody is helping me. So I asked him to suggest a security company.'

'Please come to the station immediately,' requested the woman on the phone.

'Certainly,' I replied, amazed at the sudden urgency with which my concerns were being dealt with.

I arrived at the station, and immediately felt the same feeling of dread overwhelming me.

Two female police officers escorted me into the now-familiar interview room.

Instead of asking me about being stalked, they asked me why I had contacted the supermarket owner.

I explained that I was afraid. I explained that I needed protection. I said that I had handed in an eleven-page statement that detailed all the things that had happened to me.

They looked at me dubiously.

'The next time something happens,' one of the police officers said, 'let *us* know.'

'I have tried to let you know, but nobody hears me,' I said.

One female police officer gave me her card and told me to email her. I felt utterly deflated, again. It felt a bit like they were saying, 'Don't be bothering the nice supermarket owner, he has enough on his plate.'

The nice supermarket owner was someone who had responded normally, instead of dismissing my concerns.

What was it about a man's voice versus a woman's voice that made the difference between being heard and being dismissed?

I felt utterly deflated. I could not face a repeat of this experience so I dropped the quest for private security. The familiar feeling of erosion started to pull at me all over again.

JACARANDA HOUSE

There are days when I feel like crumbling, like cliffs scooped out wave after wave, eroding me from the inside out. On those days, I go to Jacaranda House.

Seated in the large garden, surrounded by roses and tall jacaranda trees, I feel safe again. I learned this intervention some years ago. Stumbling across a podcast by Chris Germer, I was entranced by the simplicity of it: just a fifteen-minute window into a place that brings a feeling of peace.

Since then, I have gone to Jacaranda House often. I visit my grandmother as she sits on her rocking chair, knitting needles by her side, large balls of wool at her feet. We take a walk out to her rose garden, her blue wicker basket hanging loosely on her arm. In this place I'm old and I'm young. When the basket is full, we stroll slowly to the kitchen and place the flowers in various vases, tall and elegant, pink and blue glass.

I visit this place, the place of my childhood, again and again and again.

You need a place to go if your safety is compromised. You need to find a place in your mind that nobody can enter, nobody can steal. Part of brainwashing, of intrusions like this, is to gain control of the mind of the victim. 'Build a levee deep inside,' sings Natalie Merchant. My weaponry is unusual. I use music, a song, a verse, and I go to Jacaranda House, every day.

It's soothing: I come out and I have delicate purple jacaranda flowers dusting the ground in front of me. I have the smell of loamy soil and the heat of the baking South African sun on my skin.

My grandmother passed away in 1986. Years later, I passed by the huge jacaranda trees, purple flowers strewn below, the pods lying, split open, shattered by the fall from the high branches.

I don't know why, but I ended up at the front entrance of the house. It was 2002 and it had been nearly twenty years since my grandmother died, and the house sold to the highest bidder.

I felt a dull ache of sadness, sitting outside the familiar entrance to the long driveway. Nothing had changed. No tree had been cut down, no plant had been moved or dug up. There was still no fence around the property. It was as though time had stood still. The red-bricked house was still the same. Nothing had been altered and the smooth tarred entrance to the house was just the same as it had been twenty years before. In my mind I saw my cousins and I tearing down the driveway on roller skates, my aunt chiding us, my grandmother looking on, smiling.

I rang the doorbell. A friendly voice answered, 'Yes, how can I help you?'

'My grandparents used to live here,' I said. 'I miss them. I was wondering if I could walk around the garden.'

I was aware that she might laugh at me and tell me to go away. But she didn't. She opened the door and smiled broadly. 'Yes, of course you can. Come in.'

I walked down the hallway. The soft, blue carpet was almost like the one my grandparents had had. The layout of the house was still the same.

'We have visitors,' she explained. 'Just make yourself at home and take as long as you need.'

I was touched by her kindness. I felt like crying but I didn't. I stuffed down the sadness, the dull yearning, the grief, as far as it would go, till it was almost invisible. Almost.

Making my way around the garden, I saw the tree house perched in the same place. The rose gardens were still there. The bed of lilies, Zantedeschia Aethiopica, still there.

Even the vegetable garden was the same, or similar; the neatly ordered rows of baby carrots and tomatoes, beans and baby gem squash all occupied a familiar place in my grandmother's garden.

After an hour, the pain in my heart became unbearable, and I thanked the woman with the broad smile and quickly left the house.

Grief is a strange thing. It sits just beside me, walking with me during the day, like a shadow. I am not sure if I will ever stop missing my grandmother. I feel her presence most strongly on days when I am falling, on days when Liam and his participants are working hardest to crush me into the soft earth, on days when I feel so alone.

Those days I feel her arms extended, protective, warm.

IF I CAN'T HAVE YOU, NOBODY CAN

By spring 2021, I had decided to take steps to move on with my life. I'd signed up with a matchmaking service, and in mid-April the woman in charge emailed me. She told me she had found someone perfect for me. She sent me some information and a photograph of the man.

I found myself responding rapidly to her email. *Yes,* the email said, *yes I will certainly meet this person.*

I met N in Brown Thomas at the sunglasses section. It was a bright, warm summer day and the city was ebullient. Even the side streets seemed to be smiling. We spent a pleasant afternoon walking around the buildings of Cork. On the third floor of the parking lot, we exchanged a fleeting kiss. It was a sign of things to come.

He ran down each floor, waving at me on each level, like a child waving at a balloon.

Sweet, I thought, smiling as I drove home.

I knew that we had been watched, and closely monitored during the date. He didn't, of course. What a way to start a date: 'By the way, I hope you don't mind, I'm being followed by a group of people you wouldn't want to introduce to your mother, and my ex is a psychopath who is obsessed with me and sends people to stalk me. That ok with you?'

So I said nothing and hoped he wouldn't notice.

The next week we spent another beautiful summer day in East Cork at the local driving range. I'd never played golf before and we laughed as the balls spun violently outside the driving range, burying themselves in the thicket surrounding the field.

It was going well. Lunch was followed by a drive around the country and another kiss. This one was deeper, more urgent. He was exciting to be with, and it was good to feel like a woman again. He smelled faintly of pine trees and lime, and it was intoxicating.

By the third date I could tell this could go somewhere. Trips to the city, brilliant sunshine, waves and warm water on a long strip of beach in Kerry are all etched into my mind. After a day together, driving up to a lake in County Clare, I told him that I was being followed. I mentioned it to him cautiously, vaguely. I wanted him to know but I didn't want him to run away.

He seemed concerned, but we made plans to spend a long weekend together, somewhere nice. Somewhere away from everything.

One evening, returning home from one of our dates, N said, 'I came home and found things had been moved around in the flat. I have four candles on the windowsill. I know I put them there. When I got home they were gone.'

I was stunned. It was happening.

'Have you told the police?' I asked.

'No, I don't want to do that,' he said.

'You should tell the police, it could be the same people following me.'

He seemed evasive.

Still later, N said that he was followed home one evening. The next evening he took the backroads into his town and the following stopped.

N described how he found his car door open one morning, although he knew he'd locked the car.

His refusal to go to the police started to frustrate me. Things started to fall apart.

My daughter and I decided we needed a break. We drove up the Connor Pass and around to Cloghane. The high, narrow road leading up the pass was dotted with sheep. The play of light on the valley below was captivating, swirling greens changing in hue with the passing clouds. I forgot, almost, that there were people following me. That there were people out there who wanted to hurt me and hurt her.

Cloghane was exactly as I remembered it from years before, when we would rent a small cottage on the narrow road leading to the beach. The owner would always leave a dozen eggs and a bottle of red wine on the table. I would imagine she still does.

The tranquil spaces seeped into my frazzled mind and for a while, it was calm, unhurried, quiet.

I didn't want to go home. I didn't want to turn around and find the main artery leading to Cork.

Once we were back home, N said he wanted to talk to me.

I was confused by his new approach to me. It seemed different, rehearsed. He asked me how the weekend was, and I told him. He asked me where we went, and I told him. He nodded his head up and down encouragingly. 'Yes, yes,' he said.

Something told me he knew where we were. He seemed to know the answer to the questions he asked me. I couldn't help feeling that it was a test. He mentioned he knew a private detective in passing, and that he had talked to him about my situation.

The memory of my encounter with a private detective glided into view. I shuddered. Maybe his private detective had followed me, establishing credibility. A wave of fatigue passed over me.

I was really tired of this game.

A short while later, N appeared vague and disinterested, increasingly detached because of what was happening, and eventually, we stopped talking.

The thing that I had always felt had proved to be true, over and over: that whoever I was involved with, wherever I went,

Liam would do whatever it took to drive that person from my life. This was just one more example of that.

Deep down in the sinkhole of his mind, his delusional, obsessive way of thinking, he felt he owned me, possessed me. He was committed to the relationship, using others to control me.

If I can't have you, he thought, *nobody can.*

THE GOLF COURSE

At the same time that my brief relationship with N was disintegrating, I noticed a change in the air. Things had escalated again. There was more and more tapping on the roof at night. I would arrive home and often find items moved around, as though someone had come into the house and wanted me to know that they had been there. It seemed like the orchestrated, intrusive, and predatory behaviour of some gutless individual who had been told what to do. I imagined them taking refuge in the nearby shrubs, laughing at the pointless evil of their actions.

Trying to take my mind off the horror of my existence, I decided to write a few songs. It gave me a feeling of satisfaction, a quiet refuge and a moment of calm.

One morning, enjoying the peace, the horse chomping at the long grass in the field nearby, I sat at the small outdoor table just next to a small garden and began to write.

A gunshot ricochet through the air. Startled, I jumped up and looked around.

A pellet had landed close by, lodging itself in the wooden door frame. It was small, round, not a regular bullet, more like a pellet or shot used to kill wild birds and small animals. The direction it came from was the golf course. *Is someone actually shooting at me?* I wondered. Was it mistakenly fired in my direction? It seemed to have missed me by a metre or so.

I moved indoors and left the front door ajar. The golf course was of course closed and had been so since the start of COVID-19.

The open fields and hedgerows were overgrown, forming a thick boundary wall around the course. I thought about the possibility of someone out hunting. What were they hunting? And if it was a bird they were after, surely they would have seen me on the front porch, and avoided taking the shot?

But they had taken the shot and it had landed nearby. A direct aim and a near miss. Stunned, I contemplated the fact that someone was actually wanting to harm me, possibly kill me. I picked up the phone to call the police. I imagined the ensuing conversation.

'I think someone took a potshot at me today.'

'Do you have any proof of this?'

'Yes, a pellet landed in the doorway.'

'It was probably a mistake from a shooter on the greens.'

That same sinking feeling arrived, drowning me, silencing me, bit by bit. I decided against making the call and put the phone away. By now, I had had these kinds of conversations time and time again with the police, and even though it was a life-or-death situation, I could not put myself through that again.

Later that day, I tried to return to the task of writing a song. All I could hear was the ping of the shot as it landed. Had the person responsible for that aimed more accurately, I could be dead or seriously injured.

THE EFFORDSTOWN EARTHSTATION

I decided to change my morning running route. I found a road near the house that seemed quiet and narrow, and, desperate to escape the cars following me, I started using it. I found I could vanish from the world for a while, gradually going further and further each day, enjoying exploring the terrain around the neighbourhood.

I should have stayed on the roads better travelled, but I didn't. The adventurer in me wanted to go further and further. *Here,* I thought, *I would be left in peace.* Here, I convinced myself, it was hard to track someone without it being visible and obvious. I would be safe.

Occasionally, a truck from the nearby quarry rumbled past, up and down the potholed road. They turned up a steep hill, just past the Effordstown Earthstation, a name which always filled me with awe. The things they must see, peering deeply into space, surrounded by inky blackness.

One afternoon, returning from a run, enjoying the quiet hum of birds, treetops brushing the sky, I heard the high-pitched sound of something flying very close to my throat. It sounded like a sharp object being thrown. Something sharp and something round, making a high whirring, spinning sound. The sound of metal, the sound of danger.

I stopped, and peered into the thicket, impenetrable and green. Not able to see anything I bolted home, running faster and faster, breath moving faster and faster in and out of my body.

Go! Go! Go! I was saying to myself, loudly.

Arriving home, my legs were shaking. My chest was tight, heaving with the long run home at speed. I sat down on the sofa and breathed heavily. *I'm safe,* I said, over and over again.

The sound of a blade spinning close to my throat stayed with me.

Was that real? Did I imagine that? Was that just a sound or did someone actually throw a sharp object at me, missing my throat by millimetres?

I never went back on that road again, and moved out of the cottage a few weeks later.

PART THREE:
THE REAL SUZANNE

DON HENNESSY AND THE BIG REVEAL

I moved from my cottage in the country to the city. I hoped that this would stop the stalking, but it didn't. Being driven to despair by the stalking and the sea of random (mostly) men invading my life and mental space, I looked at the September 2021 programme of online and live events in Cork. I needed something to help me cope with what had been happening.

'Protection Counselling with Don Hennessy' jumped into view on the third page. Protection. That word again. I needed that, even if it was in relation to helping others.

I needed every bit of advice and wisdom on how to make that word a tangible presence in my life. I felt I had inhabited a world of terror, or that world had inhabited me. I needed help.

Walking into the long, spacious conference room a few weeks later, I let out a sigh of relief. Here were other people also needing protection, or wanting to know about being protected, or wanting to help others feel protected. Don's voice was soft and calming. I was immediately reassured. Here, finally, was someone who could help me. After two days of using terms such as coercive control, gaslighting, stalking, and mental and emotional abuse, I knew that this was the territory I needed to be in. I approached Don to see if he could provide additional support once the conference had finished. He agreed and a few weeks later, I found myself in his counselling room, tucked away in the same town where I was working as a psychotherapist.

I nervously stared at the floor. Breathing in deeply, I cautiously began my explanation of what was happening to me and around me, terrified that at any point I could lose track of my thoughts, my narrative shattering into a million pieces, words left discarded on the floor.

'I'm being followed and stalked by a large number of people,' I said carefully.

I paused, waiting for the usual response. Some sign of disengagement. Some sense that he thought I was mad.

'Yes,' he said.

'It began two years ago,' I went on, 'after a break-up. My car is tampered with, my therapy office is being broken into, things are being moved around and placed where they should not be.'

Still nothing except an encouraging expression.

'I think it's been instigated by an ex. He is a therapist, a counsellor, he lives in the area. I think his friend is in on it too. He is also a counsellor.'

At this point, I was usually stopped, and asked what proof I had of these thoughts.

'Go on,' he said.

So I did. I began telling him all about the past two years, how this bizarre and frightening series of events of intrusive behaviour, obsessive behaviour, dangerous behaviour was relentlessly directed at me. After about fifteen minutes, Don held up his hand and said, 'If I tell you a surname, will you just say yes or no?'

I froze. Stunned into silence, I nodded.

He told me Liam's surname.

A cold shudder moved up and down my spine. Like something calling me, it sent a deep shiver all over my body. My legs started to shake, and tremble. I couldn't stop shaking. Don seemed unperturbed. He sat, calmly waiting until I could speak.

It took a few minutes for the shaking to stop.

'How did you know?' I asked incredulously.

'This is not the first time I have heard of these things happening, and this is not the first time I have come across this family,' he said. 'They are known for this. I have helped a lot of women in a similar situation to find safety from them and people like them. The three brothers are all the same. They are all evil.'

I felt a wave of fear as he pronounced that word. Evil. It's a strong word. Don is a man that has seen it all. He has worked with people who abuse women for many years. For him to say that the brothers were evil meant that they were exactly that: evil.

He continued. 'They are all known for their cruelty.'

I thought of the dogs shut in the small shed during the heat of the summer, begging to be let out. The crows caw-cawing at the edge of the gaping hole at the foot of his front door. The strange feeling I'd had anytime I visited the farm, a perennial sense of fear.

I had no words. After all this time of feeling so terrified, someone was calmly asserting that not only did they know who was perpetrating this type of violence, but that they had heard a similar story many times before, all pointed at the same family.

It was growing late, and my time was nearly up. At the end of the session, Don suggested I meet with the middle brother's ex-wife to talk to her. He had helped her leave the marriage years previously. I readily agreed.

I walked out of Don's counselling room that day in a daze. It all took a while to seep in. All of a sudden it made sense. The way in which this was orchestrated demanded far more than one person. It needed a team of people. Now that I knew that the three brothers were all of the same ilk, I understood what had happened. It was as though a beam of light had suddenly been switched on in a very dark room.

I understood why his comments about his work with clients seemed so fake, so unreal, why his comments about being heartbroken seemed practiced and rehearsed. It was all to cover up who he was.

Things changed after that visit to Don. I felt that I had finally been given the gift of validation, of someone else saying, 'Yes. This is happening. Yes, you are right in what you have been saying all along. You are not the problem here.'

*

It was my second visit to see Don. He spoke in his soft, kind voice. His eyes were intelligent and alert. He heard about the ways in which I was being followed, endlessly stalked and placed under continual surveillance. He heard of their desperate need for control and the slow way in which this had all started.

The word he had coined to describe these people was psychephiles, and it was a good word, although deeply unsettling. Don, through his work with perpetrators of abusive intimate relationships, had delved into the muddy, murky depths of a psyche mostly hidden from view.

He had coined the phrase 'psychephile' to describe the personality of the three brothers. How they would befriend a woman in order to establish, intensify and maintain control of another adult. Don explained that these were the ultimate con men: liars, forging their way through life. They wanted to be liked, they did not want their true selves to be known, their true natures were always a secret. Don said they were cunning, devious abusers.

Their intention, like all other psychephiles, was long-term dominance. Their strategies, he said, were hidden from view at the start of any relationship.

He called them sexual predators. These were the people following my daughter, watching her, seeing her life unravel. These were the people waiting for her to leave for work and following her there, waiting outside until she left again. They had secret ways of indicating that they belonged to this group.

His kind of therapy, protective therapy, was unlike anything I had experienced. His insistence on naming and identifying clearly the mechanisms of this experience were simultaneously soothing and terrifying. He helped me see how these men were concealed beneath a veneer, beneath the pretend world they made for themselves. I could sense that Don was helping me out of a dark cave and he had the light. He shone it on different aspects as we made our way out of the long chamber.

His words echoed and echoed in my mind. He described the strategies used to bring women under control. Don said skilled offenders wanted to be liked, they wanted to be believed, they explained themselves by using past experiences. This was meant as an excuse, and we excused them. The skilled offender lied, and had an extraordinary skill in lying, concocting a new reality, an exaggerated and invented story in vivid technicolour. I recognised that my life had been re-imagined by these people. This was a means of control, all the lies amounting to a version of suitable reality.

I told Don of my attempts to be heard. To be heard by the judicial system, to be heard by the police. I could tell he had little time for the processes that tended to serve men over women.

We walked on and on in the cave, but the words he said, and his reassuring smile, and his insistence on using clear and unambiguous language, was soothing. It was soothing because each word was like a firefly, glowing.

It was a secret language, a code that had been concealed from view. Now that I had seen it, I could never unsee it.

It would be with me forever.

ANITA

After my first meeting with Don, he made contact with Anita. She had been married to Liam's middle brother, JJ. He asked her if she was willing to meet with me, and explained, briefly, what I was experiencing. She said yes.

A few days later, on a summer's day we agreed to meet in the wide car park of a long stretch of beach, near the small town where I worked.

We immediately switched off our phones, knowing that the conversation would be heard if we did not.

Walking slowly along the boardwalk, I tentatively asked her about her experiences with JJ that had led her to Don.

'He put a double-barrelled shotgun to my head and pulled the trigger. There were no bullets, but I didn't know that at the time,' she started. 'There were constant threats; he held my hand under a dripping pipe. The pipe had acid dripping from it. He told me that I needed to listen to him, and I did. Another time he came back from the church he'd joined in Cork city, and told me he had been chosen to lead the way. He said he could speak in tongues. He said he had been blessed. I laughed, so he beat me black and blue. Liam and their oldest brother came round and saw the damage. They seemed pleased that I had been hurt so badly. They were just standing, watching me hurt and bleeding. They were smiling. They have no conscience.'

I said that this was something I had realized over time: their lack of conscience, the way in which people are used and discarded.

'Violence is comforting to them,' said Anita. 'It makes them feel in control. It makes them feel important and powerful. They are evil.'

I could well believe that by this stage. I could imagine the joy on their faces at someone who had been bruised, battered, squashed by one of them. 'It's what we do best,' I could almost hear them say.

'The oldest brother had a dog,' Anita continued. 'He broke his leg, so the brother tied him up outside, and left a water bowl just out of reach. It took the poor dog three days to die.'

I felt sick, a cold shiver permeating my body. If they could do that, then no wonder they had little trouble inflicting the kind of damage they had done on me, and those I loved around me. It seemed that nothing was sacred. Nothing was beyond ridicule … except themselves, of course. They were beyond reproach. Beyond the rule of law, hiding behind large, electric gates where they conducted their research. Their experiment. The game, for fun, for a laugh, for money. So many willing participants, so many bank accounts being filled up, so many subscriptions.

I was the prey, they were the predators, out of sight, flawless, untouchable.

After my meeting with Anita, I thought about the whole dysfunctional family. Three brothers: unified in their quest to maximize hurt wherever possible. Their lack of remorse, the soul-less way they moved through life. I thought how the pieces of the puzzle had suddenly been put in place, and the clarity it had afforded me. I thought about the cruelty that these people were capable of, and shuddered.

ANIMALS

The architecture of their family was strange. Each of them was as depraved as the next, with individual markings of shame and rage, the perfect fuel for a fire.

I saw JJ once. Standing in a queue for a bank machine, I watched as he slowly slid in his bank card. He seemed as though he wanted me to notice him, showing the same kind of neediness that all the brothers shared. He looked very much like Liam, with the same smirk on his fat face, the same rounded stomach, protruding and falling downward. I knew instinctively who he was. He took his time, glancing furtively in my direction every now and then. He was toying with me. He was enjoying this immensely.

I wanted to go to him, to say, 'Yes, I see you. Are you happy now? Why do you want me to notice you? At the end of the day, we are both nothing. You will die. I will die. We are both of us here on earth for a limited time. Just because you think you can speak in tongues speak in tongues and feel very important in your church does not mean you are here forever. I'm glad you have money in your account. Spend it, have fun, enjoy life, you only have one. Just leave me alone.'

But I said nothing, and stared directly at the cash machine. Eventually he slowly ambled away.

*

ANIMALS

The oldest brother was a different animal altogether. I had always got the impression that even Liam was ashamed of him. I never heard his name and he was a forbidden subject, taboo. He was a family member pushed to the outskirts. During our five months together, Liam never uttered his name and mentioned him only once in passing, before moving on to the next topic of conversation. *This* brother, I knew, was a cause of ongoing shame for the family. This brother was *really* bad news.

He was never mentioned for good reason.

During my meeting with Anita, I discovered that the oldest brother was well known to the police. He had tyrannized the locals, particularly elderly women, climbing up on their roofs, peering into their bathrooms to watch them undress. He had committed every imaginable kind of intrusion into another person's life. He was known to the police, but nothing had ever been done about it. He continued to harass and stalk members of his community daily, creating havoc and fear when he seized upon a target.

He was comfortable with climbing on things, climbing over things, poisoning dogs, cats, birds, watching them die. He enjoyed making people afraid, it made him feel important. He bathed once a week, keeping the same clothes on, never receiving visitors. A feral creature, born to hunt. Anything that crossed his path was fair game. His shotgun was never far out of reach, and he kept his cattle in poverty, feeding them only sporadically. In my mind's eye, I saw him at the kitchen table in his dirty house which smelled of damp and neglect. He shoved his large, oddly shaped head into the food bowl and growled. A deep, menacing growl. Coming up for air, he pulled his large hand, dirt buried deep beneath his fingernails, across his mouth, smearing the fat of the pig on his already browned and filthy sleeve.

Watching another in fear, making another person bleed, knowing that he was causing great stress and pain for any animal or human was his greatest joy. His biggest accomplishment.

*

The three brothers were now united in this particular venture, having secretly needed and wanted this all along. How thrilling to be able to do whatever they wanted and get away with it. The right people had been handsomely rewarded for looking the other way. Pay-offs, brown paper bags stuffed with cash, parcels from the delivery vans, items exchanged for cash. And people had been warned against taking action; there would be comebacks for doing anything that in any way stopped the brothers' activities.

I could imagine the oldest brother dreaming of being a soldier. He'd watch his prisoner suffer, and become emboldened as the prisoner suffered even more. The greater the suffering, the greater the feeling of peace for the tormentor … except in his dreams.

I imagined that when he dreamed, bodies, limbs, the souls of those he had tortured came to him. They mocked him, they jeered at him. In his dreams, he'd be naked, his fat body scorned and pointed at, as he ran down the street, trying to find cover. But there would be no cover.

I know I'm dreaming, he would try to tell himself, over and over again, but it would keep happening. The laughter, the ridicule.

The dream would end and he would wake, drenched in sweat.

I know his biggest nightmare, his greatest fear, was that he would be found out. His careful attempts at concealing his innate evil were vulnerable in his dreams; his greatest fear would have been enacted in such a dream.

In the true style of cowards and bullies, his brutality was driven by self-loathing and fear.

ANIMALS

I was a convenient target; he and his brothers could all inflict their collective cowardice, their shame and brutality, on me.

It left a mark.

THE PIANO LESSON

The music school was housed in a beautiful modern building, hugging one of the long arms of the River Lee. Its glass front and the constant stream of students entering and exiting the building had always filled me with awe. I saw students, shapes tucked under their arms or over their shoulders, finding their way to classes, dedicated, alert. The river flowing on the opposite side of the road gave the building a rather grand atmosphere. I had been to a few concerts at the main hall some time before. The acoustics were wonderful, the musicians superb.

On a whim, growing somewhat tired of not moving forward with learning to play the keyboard I'd bought in the summer of the first lockdown, I walked into the building and up to the registration office. I felt nervous and out of sorts. A jangling, frayed feeling that I had grown accustomed to made its presence known, making me uneasy, unsteady on my feet.

The man behind the counter was encouraging. 'Sure, fill out the form and you never know,' he said cheerily. 'We do get a large number of applications, but you just never know.'

I filled in the form, marking an x at the *Piano, Part-Time* box.

A few weeks later I was surprised to receive an invitation for an audition. This puzzled me. How could I audition for a piano lesson when I didn't know how to play the piano?

Arriving at the audition, I was greeted by two friendly faces. I felt flustered and out of my depth, a long way from my comfort zone, safely tucked behind my guitar. Here I felt exposed. Two beautiful Steinway pianos were positioned side-by-side. I wanted to be left in the room alone so I could sound out the notes individually to hear their tone, their deep resonance through the cavity of the piano.

After singing a song, clapping a number of rhythms, and humming a melody line, the audition was over. I felt relieved and happy as I walked slowly to my car, peering at the art on the walls as I made my way out of the building. Later that day, I felt a sense of excitement at the prospect of returning to start the lessons.

*

Arriving at the first lesson, I sat down behind yet another beautiful Steinway piano, still in a state of disbelief that I had been granted access here in the first place. The piano teacher went through the book that I had bought for Grade 1, picking out different pieces to play. We started talking about music. Jean started to play his own composition. It was a piece called 'Stars'. I watched his hands criss-cross the keyboard deftly, gracefully.

Midway through the piece a searing pain jabbed at my heart. Tears pricked at the corner of my eyes. I wanted to sob, wail, empty out all of my sadness, empty out all of my fear. It was so sudden, so sharp, I had to steady myself for the remainder of the piece. Hauntingly beautiful, moving; a restless piece.

We were talking about composers, about music pieces, about melody lines. Mumbling something about jazz and folk, I tried to soothe the pain in my chest. It wouldn't budge. It gnawed at me for the rest of the day, and the rest of the following day. A deep, immovable sadness that had woken from slumber and refused to return to sleep.

I knew why it was there, but it was inconvenient. I was adept at tucking my feelings out of sight, revealing nothing of their depths. And yet, here they were, almost on display, in the middle of a piano lesson. It was not what I had hoped for.

Each lesson brought its own new angle into my heart. The weekly lesson was now infused with grief as everything I was trying to hide from welled up. Outside, my life was in ruins. Here, behind the Steinway, listening to this music, I began slowly to heal. It was not important that after the lesson the same stream of people would follow me, the same intrusions, the same smallness, the same evil would follow me.

In here, I was softening, the music floating over me like a healing balm, pulling at the edges of my frayed nerves, settling me and resetting me to face what was waiting for me out there. This was my therapy, my way of coming back.

I was slowly beginning to make sense of the piano keys, my hands learning how to curve and sound out the notes. Progress was slow; the mechanics of the instrument felt alien and difficult to grasp. It didn't matter. All that mattered was being here, out of reach, sheltered.

AN INTERRUPTED SEARCH FOR A JOB

By the middle of 2022, I was starting to feel that I needed to leave my private practice.

It was becoming more and more difficult to do my work effectively, as I became increasingly worn down and exhausted. The brothers and their network were stealing away my professional life, bit by bit, day by day.

Over the next few weeks, I gradually closed my private practice and moved from my office – with the room overlooking the garden and the company of my colleagues – in the hope that they would leave me alone. Even this did not stop them.

Having made the decision to leave, I was now in the uncomfortable position of needing to find a job. The financial pressure that I found myself in was crippling at times. I applied for positions in every field; part-time, full-time, whatever was available.

After a few seemingly successful interviews which each held the promise of a new job, a new direction and a regular paycheck, the words, *I'll call you on Monday; I'll call you; I'll call you on Tuesday,* seemed never to materialize.

I had learned not to take things too personally. There were jobs for me and there were jobs I would not get. But the silence was deafening. Something was wrong.

I pictured the brothers, rubbing their hands with glee, instructing the rather overzealous cybercriminal and co-offender in the shed outside that he needed to capture all of my emails and attempts to find work and annihilate them, one-by-one. Perhaps they'd pretend to be the police, devising a strategy to lie about me and put any potential employer off the idea of employing me, even if I would have been the right fit for the position.

The bills increased, the pressure mounted, the attempts to find work became frantic. With the extent of the brothers' network, it was me against hundreds, thousands. Another call was made; another job interview crushed. And so it continued.

The combined effect of leaving my psychotherapy practice and the silence following each interview I attended was draining the last reserves of my bank account. When I did miraculously find myself invited to an interview, I could tell there had already been lies spread. It was a done deal before I could even try to explain myself.

Feeling brave, I mustered up the courage one cold December morning to go into a few shops to see what work options there were. I struck up a conversation with a woman in a large fabric warehouse and she told me there would be work opportunities opening up soon. I had a look around the vast array of fabrics and thought that this would be a perfect place to work. Hidden from the insanity out there, I could be lost amongst the large rolls of velvet and satin, cotton and silk.

A few weeks later, I received a call. It was an invitation to have a trial period in the shop. The first two days went well. It was busy, chaotic at times; I emerged from the day covered with bits of fabric and thread. *This is great,* I thought. *I've found a job in a place I could grow to really like.* Finishing up my second day's work, I returned to where my handbag was stored at the back of the shop, opened it and took out my car key. It was bent, almost in half at a right angle, and stared back at me as I placed it in the palm of my hand. *How on earth did it become so bent?* I wondered. It's hard to bend a key. You have to really want to bend it. You really have to have the right tools with which to bend it, and the time in which to do so. This was not an accident. It was a warning.

A few days later I arrived at the shop, having not heard from the manager about future work. Her eyes did not meet mine.

She avoided me as I hovered about the front desk, and finally turned to me. 'We are, um, going to, um…' She faltered. 'We are, um, going to try out someone else.' She hurriedly moved on to the next person.

She had, of course, been bought. Or lied to. Or threatened. One of the three. That familiar feeling arrived as soon as I realized what had happened. She had been co-opted to the cause and I had once again become the problem. And I had lost my once-promising job.

I left the shop feeling deflated. In my head I heard cliffs falling into the sea, stone by stone, breaking on the surface far below. I felt eroded.

The roar of a motorbike accompanied me out of the shop. It sounded triumphant, a collective roar from the three brothers, thrilled that they had ejected me from my job, again, and that they were achieving, gradually, what they had set out to do years ago.

I remembered Liam's words: 'This therapist likes to play.'

*

The next interview had a similar theme. The man in the furniture shop seemed to know all about me.

'You seem like a piano-playing woman,' he ventured. I stopped. He went on to go into too much detail about his life, opening up about his son, his wife, while making pointed statements that implied he knew details about me. Or rather he had been told about me.

The next and the next interview, each one arrived and passed. 'We'll call you,' they said, and never did.

The smell of slurry had invaded every corner of my life and nobody was doing anything to stop it.

THE REAL SUZANNE

It was time for my regular visit to Don Hennessey. I awaited my turn outside his house. I was anxious, a jangle of nerves; my week had been long and I had had no peace at the end of the day.

It was a late appointment and the sky was full of rain. Big, pelting raindrops hammered the surface of the car. I wrapped up in my warm winter coat, wishing I had brought a scarf with me.

Once the session began, we explored ways for me to connect to things that gave me energy and that made me feel good. I found this process calming. I told him the journey my life had taken me on so far. The things that had been good, the things that had been difficult.

'I want to see the real Suzanne emerge,' he said. 'You have been pushed down for too long now. Where is the real Suzanne?' I was taken aback by his question, but I knew what he meant.

The real Suzanne had become cowed and unwilling to fight back, afraid of the brothers, afraid of everything. I knew he was calling on the part of me that had become silenced and diminished.

'I want to help you find ways to recover the real Suzanne,' he would say.

This became our goal. The goal of our work was not to stop the stalking. That was only something that law enforcement could do. The goal of *our* work was entirely to rediscover and reinforce the Real Suzanne.

Over the hour, I started to relax. The fear in my body started to seep away. I was calmer, more resolute. The ever-present harassment and stalking over the week had made it impossible to focus, but now, gradually, a soft focus returned.

During this appointment, I learned how other people Don had helped had similar experiences. They had been targets of the same people, or different people equipped with the same way of concealing their real motives, their true identity. Masks of various shapes and sizes offered a way of being who their partners wanted them to be, albeit temporarily.

I heard how one woman was being followed, in the same way, by a group of people, on walks, to coffee meetings with friends. I heard how she had developed her own code of confusing these people momentarily. But she could not make them vanish entirely, and they persisted and persisted.

Perhaps it was a widely-known and frequently performed activity. A secret activity shared by only those with a dark mind and access to the dark web. That, and lots of free time and an empty bank account in order to be available to do the stalking. A multitude of grievances, and a will to seek revenge.

What was happening to me was a framework for a much bigger picture. Framing the acts of violence, understanding the perpetrators in this way, I was beginning to see that this was also sexual predation.

Don explained that what happens so often is that we look for an explanation for any abusive situation by analyzing the behaviour of the victim, and in so doing, we collude with the abuser. He said that this collusion is the lifeblood of the offender. I thought of the many times I had tried to make myself heard, and failed. How easy it had been to make me the problem, instead of Liam and his brothers.

At the end of the session, I knew that Don had once again shone a light in the dark for me. I left the session with a flaming torch out into the dark, wet night. I was slowly gathering all the unravelled bits of myself again. Round and round, like a large ball of wool, I was wrapping them up so I was no longer so loosely holding myself together.

My visits to the police had felt like I was expelled onto the pavement, a flattened, discarded object.

But for now the unravelling was being temporarily stalled and slowed.

I knew that morning would come, and the gradual erosion would start again, but just for a few moments I was on solid ground.

RAGE

A while after moving to Cork City, having reported numerous crimes to the police, I decided to make one final attempt at making myself heard.

By now, I knew the psychological processes involved in the mind of a stalker. The predatory nature, the narcissistic merger, the self-object diffusion, the obsession. I knew the clinical assessment. I knew that this world that they occupied was the kind of world where there were no equals, only predator and prey. I knew about proxy stalking and I knew about psychephiles.

I decided to talk to someone in the police station about everything, and after a brief chat with a local police person, we agreed that I would hand over all the information I had already given countless times to the police. *Surely this time,* I thought to myself, *surely this time they'll understand what I'm trying to communicate.*

The next day, armed with folders, files, names, dates, and hope, I parked outside the local police station, and waited until it seemed quiet. I gathered my thoughts, breathed the crisp spring air deeply, and walked quickly to the station. After a brief chat, I returned home and waited for a response.

Days went by and I didn't hear anything.

That sinking feeling, the feeling of being flung out onto the pavement, was starting to return.

I asked to see the police officer and arrived at the police station later that day. I could tell something had changed. His attitude towards me had shifted. He stood, immovable, in the centre of the station as if to say *You are not welcome here.* He did not show me into the interview room, but stood just inside the door.

He started. 'I have read your notes, but you don't have any proof.'

A strange feeling started to emerge from deep within. Something stirred.

'In my notes you can see that I did have proof but needed the police to do their bit in investigating it, which they never did,' I said, trying to stay calm.

The emerging feeling was rapidly changing shape. Instead of flattened, it was starting to feel like rage. *This is inconvenient,* I thought. I tried to shove it back down but it would not go. It was rising and rising and rising fast until it almost reached my throat. I noticed that my breathing was rapid, my heart racing, my fingers clenched, sweat was starting to gather in the palms of my hands.

He started to round on me; that familiar strategy of backing someone into a corner and leaving them there. In his mind, I was the problem.

His eyes narrowed, gazing straight at me, mouth set into a downward curve. 'Well, we can't do anything unless we have proof.'

By then it was too late. The rage at not being heard and understood that had been stuffed down over the past three years had been let out.

'How can I have any proof when you never help me?!' I was yelling, I was beyond any level of anger I have ever felt. My feet were floating, I had left the earth. 'You are tying my hands behind my back, throwing me overboard and expecting me to swim!' I yelled. 'How can I prove anything when you will not help me? There are so many people who know about this, it would be easy for you to do something to stop it. There is so much information out there, so many people involved, but you won't do anything to help me. Help me!!'

Nobody moved. Nothing was said. I'd had enough.

I turned sharply and headed for the door. There was complete silence in the police station. Opening the heavy doors, I slammed them shut with all the force I could muster.

I was shaking with fury, my jaw clenched together; I was a wild animal that had been caged and shackled. I drove out of the car park, and raced home, heart banging against my chest. Bang, bang, bang, bang. The words that I had said were racing in my mind, the screams ripping open my chest had found a way out.

I had finally expressed my rage at not being understood.

It took me the rest of that day and night to settle. The boiling, seething rage would not go back inside easily. She was prowling the house, hackles raised.

That was my forty-second visit to the police station.

It was also my last.

Two days later, two policemen arrived at the house. Peering at me cautiously, they asked me if I was ok.

I wanted to laugh. I wanted to cry, I wanted to scream. 'No,' I said, trying to remain calm, 'I'm not ok.'

They seemed unsure as to what to do next and hurriedly exited the kitchen. I could see they would rather I'd lied. 'Yes, I'm fine, we are all fine,' they would have liked me to say, but I didn't.

I stared at the floor of the kitchen. Muddy paw prints from the dog decorated the white floor tiles. Piles of washing lay waiting in the laundry basket. The old Suzanne would have said *yes, yes, everything is fine. Yes, I'm fine.* But the new Suzanne had emerged. I wanted to phone Don and tell him that I finally know what he meant.

That the new Suzanne had arrived, and she was not leaving.

THE DOG

I saw Don every two weeks. He was growing increasingly concerned about my safety and the safety of my daughter and suggested I buy a large dog to help protect us. I scrolled down the list of available dogs, googling which ones I would like, until I saw a beautiful German Shepherd. The woman said the litter had been sold, but gave me the name of someone who had a puppy for sale.

There was only one left when I visited the farm. The smell of straw and mud, dog food and damp fur filled the air. The puppy was not beautiful; she was a rather lopsided-looking dog, with enormous ears, flopped forward. I fell in love with her immediately and picked her up. On the drive home, she threw up all over the back seat.

It took a while to get used to being a dog owner. I found myself spending vast tracts of time out walking. The walking never ceased, and because of this I met other dog-owners and walkers who were also out in all weathers, early in the morning and late in the evening.

We all agreed being a dog-owner was a big task, but the rewards were huge. There was a lovely feeling of community amongst the dog-walkers and the dog-owners. We met in the dog park and gradually the familiarity of those arriving at the same time each day became an anchor, a feeling of connection in the middle of a profoundly isolating experience. I never mentioned what was happening to me. The conversations were cheerful for the most part, and I relished these moments of normality in the day. They set me up and made me feel less alone.

The dog became gradually more presentable. Her ears straightened, her colouring settled, and most importantly, she started to bark. I found her loud, piercing bark reassuring. At night, while I tried – mostly unsuccessfully – to convince myself that I was safe, I was gladdened to hear her bark. I loved the way she sat: alert, massive ears pricking upwards, sniffing the air. *Don was right,* I thought to myself, not for the first time. It seemed that everything he suggested was the right move, a good way forward.

This dog, constantly shadowing me, felt protective. At times she barked at strange objects. Orange cones used for parking spaces, abandoned bicycles. But mostly, she was accurate.

Over time her bark became a large growl, a snarling, warning bell. A stranger bent down to pet her and she pulled her teeth back. I apologized but inwardly I was glad she was growling. She started to bark when I was woken up each night with someone tapping on my roof. She started to bark at odd intervals through the night, and I began to wonder if she knew something I didn't. The tapping on the roof stopped and a high-pitch screeching sound began.

Because she was termed as a dangerous breed, after a while I knew I needed to train her.

The dog-trainer was a handsome Scottish man. I warmed to him immediately. The dog did not. But after a few lessons, she was more obedient, less inclined to drag me this way and that. The dog-trainer spoke in a serious, clear tone. He explained things thoroughly. I found it reassuring and the fear that was always with me stepped aside when he was there.

I was finally learning to trust my instincts, instead of burying them. I was finally learning that my intuition was worth hearing, instead of shoving it to the side. When I was out amongst people,

I paid close attention to my inner readings. *Safe, not safe, not safe, safe*, I monitored each person as they went by.

No doubt I was sometimes wrong, but the months and years of being stalked had left me with an increasingly accurate idea of who I could trust. At least I was only in the company of safe people, people I could trust. If nothing else, this experience had taught me that.

It was a hard-earned victory that had been a long time coming, but it was a victory nonetheless. I remembered Don's words: 'I want to see the real Suzanne emerge. She has been dampened down for long enough.' Perhaps that was why I started to experience this different kind of feeling, this feeling of resolve, of outgrowing the old Suzanne.

The old Suzanne absorbed things. She was easily pushed.

She was inclined towards absolute silence, or bursts of anger. The new Suzanne had something else that was surfacing.

Steel and stone. Something immovable.

ON HOLIDAY

In mid-2022, I visited a friend in Cape Town. It was a long journey, but I was glad to be there. After the stalking and the house break-ins, the lack of response from the police and the endless, wearying persistence of the brothers following my every move, I was glad to be miles away from it all. *Surely*, I thought, *they won't be following me here. It's too far away and it would take real dedication to set this up in a country six thousand miles away.*

The days were long and hot, the sky cloudless and brilliant. There were wonderful smells in the air: spices, salt, and sea spray. We spent the days exploring the multitude of beautiful places in and around Cape Town. Kalk Bay, Simonstown, Lion's Head, the Waterfront, all brimming with life. We are old friends, sisters more than friends. We walked around the city centre and had lunch in a tiny vegetarian restaurant. I was revitalized by the heat and the familiar sounds, the cacophony of different languages; some I know, some I don't.

On the second day, I told my friend what had been happening to me in Ireland. That I was afraid and that I was being stalked. She was reassuring, comforting.

'Don't worry, you're safe now,' she said.

On the third day, I felt I was being watched.

At first I questioned myself. *Surely this cannot be. Surely they would not come all this way and set it all up again. I'm imagining this. It's not happening. I'm just tired. I'm just on hyper-alert and seeing things.*

I woke up that night with a high-pitched screech in my ear. Turning on the light, I looked around the room for mosquitoes, appliances that had been left on. Nothing. I tried to sleep, but the screech continued. I was starting to panic. Not only were they following me around here, with a new set of people, a familiar pattern of obsession, a continued intrusion into my life, they were also replicating the way in which they intruded on my life, daily, hourly, by waking me up all night long.

I tried to sleep but no sleep came. Padding down the long corridor, I felt on edge. I knew there was security in the house but still, I was afraid. Only the low buzzing of the fridge took the edge off the fear.

I tried to make sense of it all and failed. In order to follow me around here, they would have had to set up this game in the same way that they set it up in Ireland.

The next day we drove along the winding roads that hugged the steep slopes of Table Mountain. It was early in the morning, but the line of traffic brought us to a slow crawl. I watched the lights sparkle and flicker way below in the vast, sprawling city. It's a beautiful place. I can never tire of it, the way that it keeps moving.

Arriving at our favourite coffee spot, we took a seat and watched the sun rise. The coffee van was perched alongside a traffic circle, at the top of a steep hill. Cyclists had parked their bikes next to the van, and the strong smell of coffee zinged in the air. The baristas had big, loud laughs. It was hard not to laugh with them. They exuded happiness, joy, and a life full of possibilities.

I stood close, allowing the laughter to seep into my skin. It was already warm, and temperatures would rise well above the mid twenties. Sweat and laughter and coffee mingled in the air. Cars sped past, endlessly. It was noisy and busy but somehow it managed to be a place of joy. After a while, we decided to leave, and I took some of that joy home. The line of customers waiting for coffee had grown longer. The baristas were still smiling and their laughter was infectious, deep barrelling laughs.

And then it hit me: The brothers and their associates didn't laugh like that.

They smirk, they laugh *at*, they do not laugh *with*.

They do not feel joy, they feel only pleased at another's pain.

When they smile, it's a calculated gesture, meaning nothing. There is nothing beneath; they do not have a true self, only a collection of selves stolen from others.

I imagined them standing somewhere, watching me laugh and wanting it to end. Envy seeping out like greed, spreading like slurry.

To laugh like this is to let go. It struck me that the brothers and their participants would never know the kind of joy that these two baristas know.

The next day, we met a group of school friends at an outdoors restaurant on a wine estate at the foot of the mountain. Tall, leafy oak trees lined the long road up to the venue. It had been five years since I'd last seen this group of school friends, but already I was comforted by their friendship, the conversation, and the laughter. These were people who really knew me. If someone offered them money to follow me around, they would laugh. If someone told them some made-up story about me, they would become protective of me.

Here, I felt protected. Here, I felt safe.

Later that year, I took a trip to Amsterdam. By then, I strongly suspected I was being followed even out of Ireland. Someone who looked vaguely familiar got off the plane ahead of me and by the time I was in Schipol airport, I knew that it was happening. Sure enough, the days that followed were punctuated with the phone in hand, that same look, that same pattern of intrusion. I didn't bother second-guessing myself. My gut told me this was happening and this time I listened. It was the same thing, the same game, orchestrated in a different country once more.

I thought of the forty-two times I had been to the police, and how, each time, they had not believed me. I thought of how many participants, co-offenders, over the space of almost four years had witnessed and participated in the game. Thousands and thousands of people knew about it.

In my mind's eye, I travelled to the furthest point of the world. The Amazon rainforest, the forests of Northern Scandinavia, New Zealand.

But chances are, wherever I go, this will follow me, until it is stopped.

A territory of obsession.

THE NEIGHBOUR

My neighbour had started acting strangely, abruptly starting conversations about abusive relationships in the middle of the day and eyeing me darkly. I started to wonder if this neighbour, like other neighbours before, had joined up with Liam and the brothers. We had lived side-by-side for a year now in a perfectly friendly neighbourly way, but the way he was behaving now seemed different, it seemed rehearsed. Just like the previous neighbour, he had been turned.

I wondered if this conversation (or more accurately, monologue) had any point besides insinuating that I was well-versed in the language of abusive relationships. It was a blunt instrument and I turned away after a few minutes, bored by the laboured tone of his attempt.

A few weeks later he tried again. This time he put on a nonchalant, even up-beat, tone of voice.

'Come over and chill out in the lounge, if you'd like,' he said with fake friendliness. *Chill out in the lounge,* I repeated slowly to myself. Having never set foot in his house, and now having noticed a certain change of tone around him, I knew *that* would never happen. 'Yes,' he ventured further, 'we have a cozy fireplace and we always have an open door.'

Bemused, I nodded my head in what could have been agreement. 'Sounds great,' I said, and turned to walk away.

He was not very good at the game. He didn't have the edge that my first neighbour had. I listened closely to my body's response.

It said nothing. A poor man desperately clinging to an idea that he might, after all, have a part in a big play. He might become important.

He had been emptied out and in his place they had put someone else, a yes-man who did what he was told with no sort of agency.

It was a strange and interesting phenomenon to observe as it unfolded. He did not have that animal way about him, like the other predators that played this game. He was too clean-cut.

My neighbour had become a pawn in a game, and he had done so willingly, presumably being paid for his services.

*

A few days later, my neighbour received an oversized creepy shed.

'A family member asked, 'What's the deal with the new shed?'

'I'm really not sure,' I said.

'Probably to store the dead bodies,' she replied.

The remark was not made in jest. She was not laughing. A vague sense of unease settled on the conversation.

'Probably to store lawn mowers,' I said, trying to steer the conversation away.

Her comment rested like a heavy weight. Something had been said that could not be unsaid. We had agreed without agreeing that the shed was a harbinger of bad news.

A CIRCLE OF FRIENDS

Late one afternoon, an unexpected burst of rain emptied out on the streets of Cork, leaving bedraggled commuters scrambling for umbrellas or an overhang under which to shelter. I was drenched, soaked head-to-toe by the abrupt downpour.

Having parked out of town, I had a long walk and needed to dry out for a while. I made my way to the massive gothic arches of the church along the river. Its huge spires reached up and outwards, grabbing at something, while simultaneously peering down at the small figures hurrying to and fro along the sidewalk. It was an old church, and a beautiful one too. I had been there many times before, mostly to stare at the stained-glass window, tall and magnificent, the colours deep and resonating. Every small sound was magnified. Every whisper carried upwards, echoing around the vast ceiling, before returning to the atrium below.

This time, there were only a handful of people in the church. The small stubs of candles lay waiting in the large bowl near the candle holders. I took one, its smooth, waxy surface comforting in my hands. Placing a few coins in the collection box, I lit the candle and chose a space for it to burn. I said a few words remembering those I love, and those I wanted to protect, and then felt a connection to everyone and everything that was rare and sudden. It had been a long time since I had felt connected in this way. Usually I felt that I was being tormented by a gathering of disturbed people, knowledge that can make anyone feel isolated. Alone. Afraid. Now, I felt the arms of the world gather gently around my waist, settling beside me, making space in a large circle of friendship. It felt soothing, healing. To feel the whole world gathered next to you is a profoundly healing thing. The next day I passed another church, this one in my own neighbourhood, and went in. Lighting the candle, I felt the same connection; an image of all the world collectively linking arms around my waist, my arms around them, and loosely included. Not suffocating, just reassuringly held. It was as if lighting the candle had become a way into the community of the world. Like party bunting where all the flags are linked, all the people's arms are linked together, all held together willingly, closely, loosely. A friendship, an expansion.

THE DELIVERY MAN

Recently, I saw a colleague I had not seen in five years.

'Congratulations on your wedding,' she said. 'I heard you got married.' Puzzled, I looked at her to see if she was laughing. She wasn't. 'Yes,' she said, 'a delivery guy came in recently and said he was your husband. He knew all about you. He knew we had worked together, where we had worked, how long we had worked together, and he told me all about where you were living and what you were doing.'

A delivery guy. That sounded about right. The delivery vans and the delivery guys were being used continuously to harass me, to spread lies about me, and now, apparently, I was married to one of them. I thought about the research I had found on proxy stalking and multiple perpetrator stalking, and how delivery drivers were used as extensions of the primary stalker. It made perfect sense that she had been told what she had been told.

'I'm not married,' I said.

' Yes, I did find it a bit strange. I always thought that you never wanted to get married.'

I explained what was happening to me. I told her that this was just the kind of thing that was happening daily, hourly. I was being re-invented, re-imagined. I was slowly being escorted out of my life and replaced by someone else. 'They will do anything,' I said. 'And nobody is hearing me.'

She nodded her head sympathetically. She seemed concerned.

Arriving back at the car after our conversation, the faint smell of slurry filled the air. It seemed to be coming from the back of the parking lot. I saw someone sitting parked next to my car. I knew it was one of their set-ups..

I decided to film the car, the registration number, and the surrounding area. A woman walked up to me and said in a friendly voice, 'I just wanted to know if I am in your photograph?'

'No,' I said. 'The police have asked me to do this.'

'The police?' she said, sounding alarmed.

'Yes,' I said, in a matter-of-fact voice. 'I am being stalked.'

The woman looked shocked. She apologized and hurried away.

That day in the parking lot, I broke the secret net that surrounded me every day. I could see the shock on her face. I knew she believed me. I knew that she would be thinking about the woman in the car who told her, calmly, that she was being stalked.

At that moment, something changed. Some contract I had never signed was being torn up and thrown to the wind.

I drove home, elated.

This was the key. This act of unsilencing was the key to everything.

I had tried everything, and nothing had worked.

The only thing that will work is me saying these words: *I am being stalked.*

It's not a request for help, it's not a plea for sympathy.

It's a statement of fact.

PART FOUR: UNSILENCING

THE TURNING POINT

I read once that Kazuo Ishiguro always rises at 4.00 a.m. to write. I was always struck by how much dedication to his work he has. I was awake at 4.00 a.m. most nights, but for entirely different reasons. Those reasons similarly required dedication, just not from me.

I did not sleep because I was not left to sleep. Sleeping peacefully, it seemed, was for anyone but me. A few years back a man drove into his neighbour, killing him with a tractor because of the repetitive loud noise from the 'crow banger' on his farm. The two farmers had entered into what was described as a 'simmering dispute'. Eventually, a year later, the farmer who was being woken up continuously snapped. He was full of rage, and tired of being kept awake every night.

His defence was described as 'cumulative provocation'.

I could relate.

Sleep is wonderful. Who does not like an afternoon nap? Or a deep, peaceful sleep, waking to the new day, refreshed, renewed?

Once the brothers had established that nobody was going to question the neighbour, or take notes, or take me seriously, they devised even greater, more ambitious plans.

'Let's not let her sleep,' they must have said. 'Let's wake her up, night after night after night, so that she becomes even more unhinged.'

'Yes,' they agreed. ' That is a good plan. After all, she deserves it. The Grievance.

They set about their plan with the same kind of dedication they had shown for all the other plans they had hatched. The same kind of driven intensity, the same kind of malice.

In the first house it was the bang, bang, banging on the bathroom walls; a sound designed to cause an abrupt exit from dreams into the darkness of the night.

In the second house, the same intrusive noises continued. Tap, tap, tap on the roof, or on the bathroom window. It was pitch-black outside and thick shrubs and trees surrounded the property so it was impossible to see who was making the noise.

In the third house a light tapping began on my rooftop. This continued until I placed CCTV cameras all over the house. What happened next was even more baffling. Becoming used to the absence of rooftop tapping, and hoping (in vain) that this was finally the point along the journey that I could at last sleep in peace, something else began: a high-pitched, pressured screech, intruding on my dreams. It was the same sound that had kept me from sleeping in South Africa, on my visit to see a friend.

At first, I tested the appliances in my house to see if the sound was emitting from them.

No.

The smoke alarms. No.

The light fittings, the radio, the lamps, the fridge. No.

Puzzled, I tried to return to sleep. But I was woken once more, and again and again, to the sound of a high-pitched, pressured sort of noise that was audible and then faded from awareness. I felt vaguely nauseous, and found myself sweating at night, unable to sleep and on edge.

I consulted Dr Google. What makes high-pitch sounds?

Dr Google had some interesting results. It seemed that there were a variety of ways that people had employed the use of sound frequencies to keep others from sleeping or drive them away from wherever they were. I came across the 'Sonic Nausea Electronic Audible Sound Device'.

This, the website boasted, could cause headaches, intense irritation, sweating, imbalance, nausea, or even vomiting. It emitted a high-frequency soundwave, generally intended for an average-sized room.

The reviews were helpful.

'Excellent.'

'Helpful to drive away unwanted guests next door.'

'Gets the job done.'

'Is a bit like the Mosquito,' says another reviewer. The 'Mosquito', I read, was an anti-loitering device that had received mixed reviews, set up to mostly target groups of young adults.

'The Sonic Nausea Device does not seem to affect dogs or cats,' the reviews said.

I watched my enormous German Shepherd sleeping soundly and agreed.

Wikipedia added that these AHDs (Acoustic Harassment Devices) were used to stress enemies and aid in interrogation. I now understood why I could not sleep. The sweating and the tossing and turning, the nausea and irritability, would cause severe stress. Especially if you were subjected to it night after night after night.

'It could be hard to detect where these sound frequencies were being emitted from,' said the reviews. *I've got a fairly good idea,* I thought to myself.

The house was small and access points were limited. I imagined a stranger, moving stealthily through the graveyard and over the high wall. Once he was there, he would scale another low wall to find a perfectly concealed entrance point to the house behind and adjoining mine. It used to be one house, now it is two. Moving quickly and quietly, he could set up camp for the night while my neighbour slept soundly. Aiming the device towards me, playing with the frequency levels, he could receive regular updates from the brothers.

'Good work,' they might say. 'Good job. We're all counting on you.'

At night, weary from the nights of interrupted sleep and sound waves being pointed at me – with whatever bizarre instrument of torture the brothers had invested in – I moved aimlessly around the house. After numerous cups of coffee, I tried to settle back to sleep, knowing it was a futile waste of time.

I might as well do a Kazuo Ishiguro, I thought to myself.

Stunned from lack of sleep and from noise spinning in my ears, I decided to start to write about my experience.

I had written about my experiences of being watched, followed, intruded upon, on scraps of paper before, on books that were thrown in the bin, paper that was crumpled up, hastily, to avoid it being read. I had written a blog, but not published it.

I had written another blog, and had published just a few pages of writing.

That night, I decided to write a book. That night I stopped caring who saw my fear and what people thought about me. That night, I wanted to write it all and send it out into the world, like a large painting, displayed in a gallery so that people could see. I wanted to expose this big secret, this covert world of signs and signals, this psychological invasion.

That night I folded up the makeshift bed that I carried up and down the stairs to avoid being woken up at night (not that it helped) and stashed it in the bedroom. I set up a workstation and decided to write everything down, in no particular order.

As I began, a strange thing happened: I started to break free. The web that had grown so tight around me started to feel looser, and I stepped out of its grasp. After so many years of feeling bound by secrecy, bound by the constant intrusions of so many people following me, breaking into my house, watching, always watching, I now felt free.

I started to feel more engaged in things, in life, in whatever I was doing, knowing that I had this to come back to. Songs and threads of songs emerged, bit by bit; music started tumbling out of my waking and sleeping hours; I was starting to feel connected again.

I had a purpose which reflected a far greater problem. I was writing to expose this secret and to record all the forgotten and ignored bits of my past that had been disallowed and shoved under piles of paperwork slowly edging their way to the bin.

Here, finally, I could talk aloud about what had been happening silently and secretly, and have it heard and listened to. Finally I could speak without being silenced, and say everything that had been accumulating over years and years. The avoidance tactics that I had used to avoid being stalked now changed to recording events in a way that gave me peace. Even if temporary, before the next onslaught began, it interrupted a nauseating stream of intrusions.

I started feeling a sense of excitement, not just at recording events, but at the creative process of writing, of stepping into that world. I felt invigorated and determined that this secret would not remain one forever.

When I shared my wish to write a book, a friend said, 'Yes, that is something they cannot steal from you.'

I was struck by her words. How accurate they were.

Finally, I had taken control.

THE CHOIR

I decided to join a few groups and meet new people to settle more firmly into the area. At a local coffee shop, I saw a notice of a regular choir meeting. They met every Tuesday at the local GAA building.

Perfect, I thought.

I arrived at the grounds early and eventually found the choir room nestled above the main hallway. A friendly group of women soon arrived and we enthusiastically sang our way through a number of pieces. The evening concluded and I went outside, having made the usual small talk, feeling enthusiastic about the next meeting. I noticed there was a police car parked next to mine.

Climbing in the car, I smiled at the driver. I pulled out of the car park and drove home slowly. Out of my rear-view mirror I saw that the police car was behind me. He followed me to the traffic lights before turning in the opposite direction. I was surprised.

Catching myself, I wondered if I was being followed. After so many years, it was my automatic thought.

It was either a coincidence or a message: *We know you are here.*

While it *could* have been a coincidence my experience had taught me to assume the worst. If it was a message, it was made more sinister by the fact that they must have been following me. As anyone who actually knows me will say, I am the least sports-interested person in Ireland. The GAA club wasn't an obvious place for me to be.

A few months later, I found myself wondering if I was being followed again. Not by the usual participants, but by someone else.

The participants had, for a brief time, stepped back. It was very quiet on my daily walks. When I was in the city, I was left alone.

Needing to change my tyres, I drove down to the nearest tyre shop and while I was waiting in the large workshop a face suddenly popped up just opposite me. For a brief second, our eyes locked. He disappeared again. A strange feeling washed over me. I was being followed. And the reason the usual co-offenders had stepped back is because this was not one of them. This was either a private detective or the police.

I wanted to walk over to the man who had abruptly disappeared. I wanted to tell him sharply, firmly, 'I am not the problem here. You are watching the wrong person. You keep on watching the wrong person. This is not that kind of stalking. This is proxy stalking. This is multiple perpetrator stalking. The people following me are not dressed in large gray overcoats, sending me flowers and strange messages. Stop following me and start keeping an eye on the people who are behind all of this. Start watching their movements, drop in on their phone calls, watch their bank accounts, what they purchase, what the delivery van brings, who visits them in the middle of the night. You are watching the wrong person.'

I said nothing of course, and drove home once the tires had been fitted.

RED BALLOON

The movement grew and expanded as the months progressed. Some who were told lies were immune, they didn't want to be involved. Some were bought by the endlessly deep pockets of the brothers. Some had been told a creative plethora of lies and believed them deeply, fervently, finding them an even greater way to unify against someone.

They were united with Liam; they wanted to believe that he was a victim, they felt sorry for him.

Nothing could be farther from the truth, but the truth and the lies had become intertwined. The savage ways in which my life was being turned upside down and torn apart was lost entirely from view. I was a drowned voice, I had been silenced. I was an object, a thing, a beacon towards which all their pent-up frustration was aimed.

The smell of slurry spread all over the sports ground. The smell was dark, fetid, and rank.

'She is…' they whispered.

'She did…' they accused.

'She was…' they said in unison.

In a conversation with Anita, I heard how Liam had regularly harassed her when she picked up her children from school. I could hear that she too was afraid and fractured. She seemed utterly worn out.

Liam collects his son from school.

His son. The son that plays hurling.

RED BALLOON

His pride and his joy. The person on whom he has pinned all his hopes.

His son. The star hurling player.

I was starting to see how the grounds of the stadium had become the grounds for another kind of sport. A more sinister game that followed very different rules.

It was another way to make his non-existent self-worth inflate, albeit temporarily. Like a balloon, a red balloon, it rose up and up into the sky, as the boys poured out of the bus, eager to venture onto the hallowed grounds, the slight smell of slurry in the air.

The balloon rose higher and higher, out over the fields, until it popped mid-flight. The pieces fell like rain. Red rain, smashing against the hard ground, the smell of slurry exuding from where they fell.

Broken fragments of a distorted self.

I considered spreading a few bits of choice information myself, but he is a convincing liar, and a skilled manipulator of people. I would be wasting my time.

So I decided to keep my eye on my own goal: finishing this book.

PSEUDOCOMMANDO

Anita would send me bits of information about Liam and the brothers, and I would tell her information on developments at home. During our first conversation, I received information from Anita that her ex-husband, JJ, attended church and was rather a devout churchgoing man. 'In there,' she continued, 'he said he's learned to speak in tongues, and has been touched by God.'

I found this information interesting.

Returning from the city one afternoon, I passed by the church. Seeing that the doors were open, I decided on a whim to see what this church was all about. There were pamphlets neatly arranged by the door, and a man stood at the entrance. Inside the main hall, there were a few people gathered, but for the most part, the low-ceilinged building was empty. There was a strange feeling in the air. I could not name what that feeling was, but I felt uneasy. *This is a place where people are converted*, I thought to myself.

The man greeted me in a friendly manner, and we struck up a conversation.

He told me all about the church, its origins, how there was a collection for the homeless on Thursdays. When I mentioned the name of the middle brother, he seemed taken aback. Looking at me rather cautiously, I noticed a change in his tone of voice. It seemed higher now, his cheeks reddening. I got the feeling he was on guard. He acknowledged cautiously, reluctantly, that he knew this man. He was hiding something.

I asked him what JJ did in the church. He responded that he was in charge of helping people to their seats. I pictured the middle brother, puffed up with pride, finding his best shoes, digging them out of wherever he kept them, and standing in front of the old mirror, pleased with his reflection.

The years were starting to show, and his rounded face appeared puffy and pale. Bits of black hair were starting to find their way into his ears or his large bulbous nose. He would brush a bit of dandruff off his shoulder and stuff his slightly crumpled shirt over the hanging bulge of his stomach and into his trousers. On the drive to the city, he would feel buoyant, purposeful, powerful. *All these people, all these people to direct, to show, to win over and convert. The church is counting on me*, he says to himself. *I will do my best.*

I left the church feeling oddly relieved. Information is a powerful weapon. I had been told things about this man: his capacity to hurt, his empty, soulless eyes, how he tried to occupy a powerful place in his community. But the phrase that kept coming to me over and over again as I drove home, armed with this new information, was this: *They are nothing amongst nobodies,*

The conversation with the man in the church, who so helpfully described JJ's menial duties at the church, had demoted the brother, had reduced his potency in my mind.

Now he was just another criminal, just another bully, covering his own feelings of inadequacy and loneliness with rage, and a penchant for violence without being caught.

Acquiring the truth about this brother made him seem less of a threat.

That did not mean I was not afraid of him or what he could orchestrate against myself or my daughter. He, like the other brothers, was a criminal, engaged in violent, intrusive, illegal behaviour. But the information I now had diminished him in size. He seemed smaller, less powerful, more insignificant.

Pseudocommando
I drove home with a smile on my face and the radio blaring.
It had been a good day.

MARY BLACK

It was late autumn in 2022 and the new music group that I had joined at a local pub was in full swing. We took turns around the sturdy wooden table outdoors to sing and play. On these nights, I felt weightless, free, suspended somewhere between the notes and harmonies that we played. People stopped by from time to time to chat or request songs. The outdoor area was unusually full that evening. A woman stopped by the table and asked if we could play Mary Black. We told her we played a few of her songs.

Pretty soon, we were midway into 'By the Time it Gets Dark'. The woman's voice was strong and emotive. The crowd fell silent and listened intently to the song. We moved on to another number, 'Black is the Colour', and the crowd remained hushed, bursting into cheers at the end of the songs.

It was magical, a moment in time when life was richer and full of colour. The night proceeded in the same way: people arrived and left, songs were exchanged, laughter, the sense of community.

It was a sense of community that I thought I had lost. I remembered the feeling of community from before this started. How I would chat to my neighbours, how we would exchange news and gifts at Christmas, small things that made one feel at home. Moving to Cork, I had to start all over again. The slow erosion had made me more reclusive, withdrawn, less inclined to connect.

That evening, I felt I had established, even momentarily, a feeling of community again, my old self returning.

I made my way back home at the end of the night, walking instead of driving, which was unusual. It was late and the streets were quiet. Anyone watching me that evening, laughing, playing with the musicians, chatting to the crowds or making my way up the hill, guitar strapped to my back, would have imagined that life was pretty good.

Nobody would have imagined that there was something sinister that had invaded my life, the smell of slurry, the volley of lies about me, about who I was, spread around to anyone willing enough to absorb them.

Once I was home, I thought of the evening that had passed. I thought about how music had consistently propped me up and propelled me forward. During these last four years, it had been sitting beside me, like my faithful German Shepherd, shadowing me around the house. When I was at my lowest ebb, it moved into place, softening the violence of the day.

BATTLEFIELD

The next visit to Don was a difficult session. The weeks had been full of ambivalence and a marked increase in the number of people sent to stalk me. The emotional temperature of the three brothers and therefore the co-offenders was easy to read. During the times when Liam's son was playing hurling, when the trips to the large sports stadium in the city were intensified, and there was more activity around the son and his games and Liam's opportunities for vicarious glory, the network's participants were more eagerly recruited. There was a heightened sense of entitlement, a heightened sense of wanting to push me down.

It was a familiar pattern I had identified a long time ago. I found it exhausting.

I spoke to Don about the strangeness of it all: the proxy stalking, the way in which the game was being orchestrated. I spoke of my latest attempt to gain help from the police.

'They won't help you,' he said. 'They don't understand your situation and they don't really want to.'

I was taken aback by his abruptness, yet I knew he was right.

No help was coming. I would have to fight this on my own.

*

I visualized a battlefield.

On one hand, there were the three brothers, armed to the teeth. In front of them were long, thin lines of cocaine. They rubbed their hands with glee.

Next to them were their cronies. Acres and acres of participants. Each participant had a phone and was aiming it at me. The numbers intensified; there were different people from different countries. I thought of my time in South Africa and Amsterdam where the same game continued, just as in Ireland. A transportable hell.

The participants were faceless and nameless, zombie-like. They were robotic, soulless chunks of metal. The brothers, stomachs protruding, gave the command and they started to advance, grinning, mindless, towards me. It was now fields and fields and fields of automatons stretching out for miles, and the three brothers were sitting at a computer, mouse in hand, guiding their direction, telling them to move left or right and when to move. It was a slow avalanche of machines without souls directed towards me.

*

Don explained that the neighbours living near the brothers had started to complain to the police. There had been an increase in activity, hushed talks of drugs being smuggled in and out of the properties, cars endlessly coming and going. A fleet of cars, all owned by the brothers, were constantly being switched up and changed around. Various large, shed-like structures were appearing on their properties, dotting the farmlands with a familiar shade of green.

Anita mentioned the same news, of people in and out of the properties, constant movement, delivery vans, large trucks, sheds being built, a little empire growing and evolving.

'I can tell you one thing for sure, Suzanne, they are not doing any farming there. They are even hiring people to look after the cows,' she said. 'They must be very busy with something else.' She gave me a knowing look.

'Very busy,' I said, understanding exactly what was keeping them so preoccupied.

DOG INJURY

The dog grew up to be rather bigger than expected. Her large paws left muddy prints around the house; she was jubilant and overjoyed with life. The constant in and out of the house for walks left me at times rather short on sleep. But I was short of sleep anyway, so it was only a minor complaint outweighed by the joy of having her around. After a few months, she was ready to be left at home for short intervals, and we found a dog-walker to come in and take her for walks during the day. This went well for a few weeks as she and the dog-walker became friends. I received messages showing the two of them out on the fields.

One morning I received a disturbed voice note from the dog-walker. The dog was not well. She was lying on the foot of the steps and did not want to leave the house. She was listless; the dog-walker was concerned. I arrived home to find a very different dog awaiting me. Instead of her usual buoyant self, she was sleepy. I had a feeling she had been drugged. She had difficulty breathing, her breath becoming stuck in her nose, short blasts of air an attempt to expel something from her throat.

I was puzzled and alarmed. Someone had hurt her. I booked an appointment with the vet for the next day. The next day arrived, and the dog was better, although not entirely. *Maybe I'm imagining things*, I thought to myself. Surely someone would not have hurt her. Later that day I took her for a walk. She was struggling to breathe, her breath coming out in coughs. Abruptly she started to snort. She struggled up the hill to the house.

Later on in the year, I arrived home to find that her paw had been sliced in half. It looked like the work of a razor blade. She was making striped patterns on the kitchen floor, the blood patterning the kitchen lino. I wondered how someone could do this. How someone could incorporate the damaging and harming of a helpless animal into his disturbed psychosexual world.

I had heard about other victims of stalking whose pets were harmed, killed, disposed of, poisoned. It seemed to be a pattern. A way of delivering a message: *I will harm you and everything you love. I will get to you regardless of where you are because you are mine.*

This violent attachment to me was hard to comprehend. There were times when I wanted to diminish the terror of what it implied, I wanted to laugh about it, I wanted to convince myself that it was not real and it was not serious. After all, that *is* what I had been told countless times.

The therapist in me knew that he wanted me to be his, and when I had rejected him he felt shame, humiliation, and rage. The therapist in me could stand back and understand obsession. I bought books on it, to try to understand and make sense of it even more.

But beyond that, beneath that understanding, I was absolutely terrified.

MY DAUGHTER IS BEING TARGETED

My daughter was being targeted. I could see it. I could feel it.

I broached the idea with her; she shrugged it off. Probably in self-defence. Maybe anyone her age would have done the same.

The brothers were becoming more and more desperate. They had previously targeted her, but now it was with more intensity. They had been following her for months: to work, from work, outside her work, with her friends on a night out. I had watched them and I had watched her. I knew she had noticed them, but she did not want to talk about it.

I noticed small but significant things. It started out as trivial things, easy to disguise. A night out with the girls and then a day in bed, feeling ill, throwing up all over the bedspread.

It progressed: a night out followed by two days of throwing up all over the bedspread.

Then a week of feeling ill, a mysterious bug that had landed, somehow, and made her temperature spike and her stomach turn. I sometimes got the feeling she had been drugged. Her sleep at times was too heavy and she would not wake up. I would call her; she would not stir. When she woke up, she was bleary-eyed, finding it hard to shake off a feeling of heaviness, drowsiness.

I watched how these intervals between bouts of sickness became shorter, as the sickness became longer.

How does one say what is happening?

How does one broach the topic?

Eventually she acknowledged that she saw what I saw. That she heard what I heard.

'I *am* afraid,' she said. 'I push what is happening away. It's too terrifying to acknowledge.

I was becoming desperate for help. Inside I was screaming.

Inside, I was banging something hard against a brick wall and getting nowhere. I wondered what he would do if someone poisoned his beloved son, the son that plays hurling and would make him feel proud, slowly climbing the ladder to the pot of gold at the top. I wondered what he would do if someone directed that kind of violence towards someone he cared about.

He would take out his shotgun, hand it to someone, and tell them to pull the trigger. Being a cowardly sort of man, he probably wouldn't pull the trigger himself, but I could imagine he would order someone else to do it.

I imagined the brothers coming up with ideas as to how to further torment me.

'Well,' they would say, 'we don't want her to publish this book, or come close to finishing it, so we'll target her daughter, in a way that nobody will know it is us. We will make her throw up, feel ill, give her a temperature, miss work, make her feel sick. After all, there is a lot at stake here. We have a lot to lose. We have a lot to gain if we keep going.'

So they kept going. They kept making the daughter sick and the mother sick with worry and fear. They kept going, and their participants kept going, knowing that *their* sons and *their* daughters were not being targeted, that their sons and daughters could sleep peacefully without invasions into their lives and their sleep.

I wondered how the participants could go along with this, knowing what they knew. Maybe it was that to them, by degrees, I had become a non-human, and so had my daughter.

The thought was both frightening and bewildering. How could so many people agree to participate in this? What had she got to do with any of this?

But because she was precious to me, she had everything to do with this. Their plans extended to watching her, monitoring her every move, recording her conversations, watching her through the camera on her phone I have asked her to cover again and again.

It extended to her physical well-being and to her mental well-being. They were targeting her with the same violence with which they had been targeting me. They made her sick so that I was sick with worry and could not carry on life as normal.

They targeted her again and again and again, secretively, furtively, under a veil.

My daughter had been drugged. My dog had been drugged. What was the next step? Was there a point beyond which they would say, *ok, we've gone far enough?*

No. There was no such point. Why? Because this was the mentality of stalking. And in Ireland, there is no stalking law, and so there are few who understand the stalking mentality. The mindset of a killer. There are even fewer who understand proxy stalking.

Does a stalker stop to consider the damage being done to the victim?

No. He carries on relentlessly. He *wants* to cause damage. He wants to be violent, this wish is rooted in his being.

This is no different. The only difference is that I must write a book on it, in order to be heard.

Maybe they are also awake right now, glued to their laptops, watching me write their futures.

Maybe for once, after a long four years, I am tapping on the walls of their minds, intruding upon the space that they had presumed untouchable.

That thought alone spurs me on.

DRUGGED

As I continue to write, as the book becomes more revealing, the violent behaviour increases. The high-pitched sounds from the roof escalate, the online stalking escalates, the proxy stalking escalates. I have a feeling that Liam and the brothers are growing concerned that I am finding a path forward, and that it includes revealing all that has gone before.

On Wednesday 23rd May 2023, after a music session, I arrived home, the songs that we had sung still reverberating around in my mind. I let the dog out and, once that was done, I flopped into bed and a dreamless sleep ensued. A long while later I was woken by the sound of my heart beating. Badoom, badoom, badoom. It was deep and loud, a warning bell from somewhere within. It had been calling me for a while, and I finally awakened, pulled from sleep.

It was the kind of fear that was one step beyond what I was already feeling. I felt frozen with terror as some un-nameable thing warned me there was someone in the house. I was in danger.

In my awake yet half-asleep fog, I tasted something in my mouth. It was a sharp mixture of rotten eggs with something poisonous, something dangerous. It was a smell that was hard to place but I knew I had smelt it before.

I had been drugged.

In my hands, folded up tightly, were the earplugs I knew I had placed in my ears the night before. They lay there, like sleeping birds, closed in a fist.

I was trying hard to wake up, to fully enter the night, but it was a slow process. My heart was thudding loudly in my chest.

I tried breathing slowly, I tried getting up, I tried sipping water, I tried to think of peaceful things, but it would not stop. The fear that was lodged in my body would not leave. It stayed there till morning, loudly, relentlessly warning me. *Someone is in your house, this is dangerous territory.*

The next day I steered myself towards the kitchen in a half-awake, numb state of mind. Mid-morning, I headed to the hardware store and stocked up on nails, thick and thin.

Returning to the house, I spent a good half-hour banging and banging at the floorboards between my neighbour's house and mine. The hollow thud of the empty space beneath the stairs rang out.

I imagined a half-human beneath the stairs, crouched, waiting nervously for the banging to stop, aware that any noise might alert the neighbour to his hiding place. I kept banging for as long as I could.

*

In my mind, I imagine the scene that has been set.

The hollow cave below is quiet. I know he is there, and that the price for breaking into the house is a well-paid one. 'There is a lot at stake here,' the brothers might say, looking at the participant, darkly, threateningly. 'The eyes of everyone will be on you. You must do this to keep our viewing rates high. Film the whole thing and we will put it on the dark web, so that all our subscribers, all the channel viewers, can watch her struggle from sleep, to the darkest terror.'

I imagine the half-human under the stairs, determined to succeed. The nails being fired into the wooden staircase above present a new challenge, but no doubt in time the brothers will find a way of bypassing that, managing to vaporize the half-human into the house by some equally dark means.

Perhaps once more images of violence, images of me, of my daughter in some distressed state, would be broadcast to the world.

*

A few days later, I noticed four large, finger-sized bruises on my upper thigh. I stared at the marks and found I was at a loss as to what to do.

The thought of going to the police made me feel ill. If I went to the police, I risked walking away with the same feeling that somehow, *I* had become the problem. That even being drugged, possibly sexually assaulted, I would still not be heard and believed.

I stared at the bruises, and then photographed them. I started to Google 'date rape drugs', then put the computer away.

In the absence of protection, there was little point in even contemplating what the bruises meant. I thought of the research I had come across, how proxy stalking meant that co-offenders were an extension of the primary stalker, and how that primary stalker wanted to maintain control and was committed to continuing the relationship. How Don Hennessy had talked about these kinds of men having the same psyche as paedophiles and how they were sexual predators, armed with a feeling of entitlement towards women, particularly in the bedroom. I thought about the dark tetrad, the mindset of a stalker, pseudocommando.

It all added up. But all the information in the world could not help me.

That was up to the police, and they were not listening.

And they are still not listening.

THE TRUTH

The brothers and their players, their co-offenders, are now at peak performance. Their frenzy to silence me, to drown out my voice, to push me down until I break, is palpable. I feel it in the morning, in the afternoon, all through the night; a will to break me into a million pieces, again and again.

This kind of frenzy is new. Somehow there are elements that have not been used before.

A madness that is hard to describe, and terrifying to experience. I am both witness and target. They turn their swords on me and I wake again and again.

If their frenzy is an indication of anything, it is this: writing this book is a threat to them. Writing this book threatens to end their four-year hold on me. It threatens to expose the underbelly of their society, the kind of person they are, and show its infested, wormy darkness to the rest of the world.

They are so united in delusion, so convinced of their lie that became reality, they will do anything to stop me from shining a light on it, from letting the secret be known.

Once it is no longer a secret, all the potency will be eroded. All their power will be stripped and the brothers and their workers laid bare. The spidery web that has been circling me for so long will be permanently broken. Hiding behind anonymity at the moment, it is only a matter of time before word gets round and true identities are revealed. Even if that never happens, hunting me, hurting me, stalking me by proxy, will not be exciting when the world is reading about it.

So I write. I write to tell my story. I write to put the marks of pain that I feel on the page, transparent, so that everyone can see. The mask I have been wearing, the concealment of my own, is gone.

Here is my fear, my ongoing terror.

Here is my pain.

Here is my story of being stalked.

Here is my exhaustion, my sleepless nights.

Here is the truth.

There is nothing I want to hide anymore, after years of stuffing down my emotions, so deep that nobody can see them. In this book, I have put them out to air.

I have put them out because they do not serve me well, hidden from view.

I have told my story because I was silenced and concealed for so long.

I have disallowed all of my inner world for as long as I can remember.

All hard lessons in life have at least one take-away. In the many lessons learned so far from this continuing nightmare, maybe this is one of the gifts offered to me:

To show how I feel and not be afraid of it.

ACKNOWLEDGEMENTS

I would like to thank friends and family for their support and understanding.

In addition I would like to thank KJ for being the unique, wonderful person she is.

To Beatrice, for her wisdom and grace, Don Hennessy, for his wisdom and kindness over the past two years and for shining a light, for his ability to name things that need to be named.

To the music group in Aghada for the laughter and learning, to the music group in Cork for the joy of playing together, to Lal for the yoga and dancing, to the running group in Midleton, to the yoga group in Aghada, to the Nia group in Midleton.

To Sally, a true sister and wonderful friend, and Mary-Ann for her friendship and support.

To Caroline for the walks and talks and encouragement during a dark time.

To my many colleagues who have stood by me all these years.

To Mary for the cups of tea and laughter, to Cathy for sharing her story with me, to Kate for all the years of friendship, to Ross who helped me tame my dog, to all of the school friends who have offered unconditional friendship all these years.

To Helen, for her kind and gentle way, to Jean for the piano lessons, to Shannon for giving me a piece of the puzzle.

To Dr J Reid Melody for his brilliant books and research on stalking.

To TK Logan for her truly helpful research and further recommendations to me

To Rebecca Brown at Pretty and Precise for her flawless editing, helpful guidance, and words of encouragement during the final stages of writing this book and to Andrew Brown for his wonderful book cover design.

To Chris Germer and Kristen Neff for the lessons in self-compassion.

Thank you to the dog owners at the Skehard Road Dog Park for the good company on difficult days.

To my clients, who kept me grounded.

And to all those who, in their own way, showed me kindness and understanding towards me these past few years.

Thank you.

ABOUT THE AUTHOR

Suzanne is a counsellor and psychotherapist. She was born in Cape Town, South Africa, and has lived in Ireland for nineteen years.

She now lives in Cork city.

This is her first book.

Printed in Great Britain
by Amazon